Narrative, Literacy and Face in Interethnic Communication

by
RON SCOLLON and SUZANNE B.K. SCOLLON
both of the Center for Cross-Cultural Studies
University of Alaska, Fairbanks

Volume VII in the Series
ADVANCES IN DISCOURSE PROCESSES
Roy O. Freedle, *Editor*

 ABLEX Publishing Corporation
Norwood, New Jersey   07648

Printed in the United States of America.

Library of Congress Cataloging in Publication Data

I. Scollon, Ronald, 1939–
   Narrative, literacy, and face in interethnic communication.

   (Advances in discourse processes, ISSN 0164-0224;
v. 7)
   Bibliography: p.
   1. Athabaskan Indians—Languages—Social aspects.
2. Intercultural communication.   3. Interpersonal
communication—Alaska.   4. Indians of North America—
Languages—Social aspects.   I. Scollon, Suzanne B.K.
II. Title.   III. Series.
PM641.S3   497'.2   81-14857
ISBN 0-89391-076-7   AACR2

                        ,

ISBN 0-89391-086-4 (pbk.)

ABLEX Publishing Corporation
355 Chestnut Street
Norwood, New Jersey 07648

CONTENTS

PREFACE TO THE SERIES

Roy Freedle
Series Editor

This series of volumes provides a forum for the cross-fertilization of ideas from a diverse number of disciplines, all of which share a common interest in discourse—be it prose comprehension and recall, dialogue analysis, text grammar construction, computer simulation of natural language, cross-cultural comparisons of communicative competence, or other related topics. The problems posed by multisentence contexts and the methods required to investigate them, while not always unique to discourse, are still sufficiently distinct as to benefit from the organized mode of scientific interaction made possible by this series.

Scholars working in the discourse area from the perspective of sociolinguistics, psycholinguistics, ethnomethodology and the sociology of language, educational psychology (e.g., teacher–student interaction), the philosophy of language, computational linguistics, and related subareas are invited to submit manuscripts of monograph or book length to the series editor. Edited collections of original papers resulting from conferences will also be considered.

Volumes in the Series

PREFACE TO VOLUME VII

This book began as a collection of articles which were written in response to pressing needs for three kinds of information. Practitioners in the fields of education, law, health, and management, both in Alaska and outside, are in urgent need of information about the dynamics of interpersonal communication, especially where this communication is between members of different ethnic groups. In our work as ethnographers, teachers, and consultants throughout Alaska, and in parts of the Canadian North, we have repeatedly found the recognition that while differences between ethnic groups have their basis in historical, economic, and political factors, these differences are largely played out in specific communications between members of the different groups, both face-to-face and written communications. As a result, interethnic communication lies at the center of most issues of social, economic, and political concern in the north today.

A second pressing need for information has come from various policymaking bodies outside of the Canadian North and Alaska. National organizations with a concern for understanding discrimination against Alaska Natives have sought materials that would be helpful in informing the national policymaking process. In seeking to be responsive to this need, we have felt, again, that communication between members of Alaska Native groups and members of other groups, both native and non-native, lies at the heart of problems of discrimination in schooling, in the delivery of health services, and before the law.

A third group which has sought information about interethnic communication is Alaska Natives. Again, many Alaska Natives have identified communication whether in English or in Alaska Native languages as being a focal issue in achieving educational equity, justice, and a viable relationship with non-native political and economic interests. Ten years ago, the Alaska Native Claims Settlement Act was enacted by Congress; and, in exchange for an enormous home territory of immense beauty and economic resources, Alaska Natives received title to some remaining lands, and a cash settlement through the established mechanism of profit and non-profit corporations. In another ten years, the interim period, during which transfer of lands and cash payments are to be completed, will expire. The reality of the situation is that Alaska Natives have been placed under strong pressure to engage the modern, worldwide corporate structure. At the heart of the engagement is interethnic communication.

It is not characteristic of prefaces to acknowledge weaknesses. The work presented here is partial and obviously inadequate to the tasks we have just outlined. It is the pressing need for information by practitioners, policymakers, and the native corporations that provides the impetus for this work. The original articles on which this book is based, as well as the new chapters now included have been written with these three audiences in mind. As a result, we have tried to achieve a balance between a scholarly presentation and a style that will be accessible to readers without specialized training in linguistics or ethnography. We hope that this accessibility to non–specialists will not constitute a barrier to academic professionals with an interest in discourse, the folklore of narrative performance, the ethnography of speaking, cognitive psychology, language development, and linguistics.

The book began as the four articles now presented as Chapters Two, Three, Four, and Six. The original titles were "Athabaskan-English Interethnic Communication," "Literacy as Interethnic Communication: an Athabaskan Case," "The Literate Two Year Old: the Fictionalization of Self," and "Thematic Abstraction: A Chipewyan Two Year Old." Chapter Five incorporates our work on traditional Athabaskan narrative performance. This work provides a parallel between the literate orientation and the oral narrative tradition, showing both the end-points (Chapters Three and Five), and the earliest patterns of socialization to these different cognitive and communicative orientations (Chapters Four and Six). Chapters Seven and Eight provide a conceptual basis for relating patterns of discourse in face-to-face communication, or in writing to values on interpersonal relationship or "face." We argue that the differences between communicative patterns in different ethnic groups are fundamentally rooted in values placed on interpersonal relationship. Our conclusion is that respect for individual difference is the key to unlocking miscommunication in interethnic contexts. We hope this book will suggest just how significant those individual differences can be.

In writing this book, we have enjoyed the critical commentary of many colleagues. Howard Van Ness, John Gumperz, and Courtney Cazden have each provided their different perspectives on this work as it was in the process of formulation. We have profited greatly from discussions with Richard and Nora Dauenhauer, often in the middle of conducting workshops in interethnic communication for various agencies within the State of Alaska. We thank Dennis Demmert for continually reminding us of the urgency and significance of these issues to both Alaska Natives, and to state and national interests.

In our linguistic work, we have learned much from Ben Marcel of Fort Chipewyan and Gaither Paul of Tanacross who have treated us with much patience and understanding as we have recorded, transcribed, and edited their stories. Eliza Jones, a linguist at the Alaska Native Language Center, has taught us much about the structure of Athabaskan languages, and about the structure of Athabaskan oral performance, as a mother and grandmother of Athabaskan children she has taught us much about both the process of socialization, and the difficulties of studying such things across ethnic and cultural boundaries. As the niece of the late Chief Henry of Huslia she has also helped us to understand the wisdom of her highly respected uncle.

Irene Reed, Chad Thompson, and Jane McGary of the Alaska Native Language Center have read many different drafts and versions of these chapters, and have always provided insightful comments.

Our fieldwork at Fort Chipewyan was supported by the National Endowment for the Humanities in Washington and the National

Museum of Man in Ottawa, and we wish to gratefully acknowledge this support. Our fieldwork in Alaska has been supported by over two dozen agencies, from school districts to native corporations, in the form of providing travel expenses and access to crucial situations in which interethnic communication is involved. We would like to thank all of these agencies for their concern for the problem, and for their encouragement of our work.

Finally, we are dependent throughout our work on the individuals, both adult and child, with whom we have worked and discussed these issues. In many villages from Holy Cross, Alaska to Fort Chipewyan, Alberta we have worked with people who have always shared their time and concerns with us. Out of respect for the privacy of these individuals, we do not name them here but we are deeply thankful for their interest in helping us to understand their urgent concerns.

Ron and Suzanne B.K. Scollon

PART ONE

DISCRIMINATION IN INTERETHNIC COMMUNICATION

ONE

THE CENTRALITY OF COMMUNICATIVE STYLE

DISCRIMINATION AS A COMMUNICATION PROBLEM

In 1978 the Alaska Judicial Council issued a report based on a study of plea bargaining. The report argued that blacks and natives in the state of Alaska were receiving longer sentences in the state's courts than whites for similar crimes. Included in the report was the suggestion that some of this disparity in sentencing was attributable to differences in patterns of communication.

Since the case of *Lau vs. Nichols*, it has been legally recognized in the United States that where the language of school children differs from that of the school staff there is a serious potential for discrimination against those children. It is the school's legal responsibility to correct this discrimination.

More recently a federal judge in Detroit has ruled that a school district must take into account the language of a child's home, even where that language is a dialect of English, in meeting federal requirements for nondiscrimination.

Social workers, economic planners, and others involved in governmental agencies, business, and Alaska Native corporations all indicate the centrality of communication to problems of discrimination. From the face-to-face employment interview to plans for regional economic development, miscommunication between

3

members of different ethnic groups is a central problem and may produce discrimination against ethnic minorities.

The issue of discrimination to a considerable extent is a problem of communication. Much of the miscommunication between members of different ethnic groups occurs because of fundamental differences in the values placed on communication itself, and because of differences in interpretation caused by differences in the values placed on interpersonal face relations. These differences are values taught to members of these groups as a significant aspect of their identity as individuals and as members of ethnic groups. The solution to problems caused by ethnic difference is, therefore, not to eliminate those differences but to cultivate a deep and genuine respect for differences in individual and ethnic communicative styles. As Erickson (1976) has argued, we must "take into account ethnic, racial, social class, and other kinds of particularistic attributes of the statuses of persons meeting face to face" (p. 144).

GATEKEEPERS AND COMMUNICATIVE STYLE

Erickson (1976) has identified the importance of gatekeeping encounters in interethnic communication. These situations are those in which some person is given the authority to make decisions that will control the social or economic mobility of another. This individual keeps the "gate" to a bureaucratic, technological, or legal institution, controlling access to this institution by all outside applicants. These encounters are focal for both the institution and the individual. The flow of personnel into the institution is controlled by such gatekeepers. For the individual, future possibilities are either opened or denied by the outcomes of these encounters, that is, by the decisions of the gatekeepers.

It is significant that gatekeeping encounters are largely structured as focused face-to-face interactions. Whatever noninteractional material has been prepared in advance, job announcements, applications, or tests, the decision rides on the face-to-face encounter. These encounters on the whole are structured to eliminate as many outside factors as possible. They are structured to create an "objective" evaluation. The interview takes place across a desk in a room or space closed off from other interactions. Gatekeepers are instructed in objectivity by both institutional policies and legal codes covering potential discrimination.

Nevertheless Erickson found significant "leakage" into these encounters of two kinds. One sort of leakage was from what he called "co-membership." In a junior college counseling interview, for example, if a counselor found that he and the student were both involved in wrestling, this significantly altered the outcomes of the encounter in favor of the student. Co-membership resulted in a partiality in favor of the student in the decisions of the gatekeeper. It is this sort of leakage that is legally acknowledged and controlled in some contexts as conflict of interest.

The second sort of leakage in gatekeeping encounters is provided by communicative style. Erickson found that particularistic indicators of ethnic identity produced some form of leakage in every encounter they observed. While co-membership had the effect of overriding leakage from communicative style, in "*no case collected* did particularistic attributes of social identity *not* affect the conduct and outcomes of face-to-face interaction" (p. 141).

From Erickson's work we conclude that in any situation in which there is interethnic communication, but especially in gatekeeping encounters, there is a serious potential for discrimination against the less powerful interactant, based on leakage from communicative style. Interethnic communication between Athabaskans and non-Athabaskans in Alaska and Canada provides a continual, ongoing potential for discrimination against Athabaskans. While this is just one example of the dynamics of interethnic communication we believe that differences in world-view are experienced as values in face-to-face interaction universally.

NARRATIVE DISCOURSE AS
COMMUNICATIVE STYLE

The world of face-to-face interaction is a full world of considerable complexity. Communicative style finds expression in everything from the rhythmic movement of the body in speech to clothing styles. We have chosen to use just one aspect of this totality to illustrate our case. We have chosen to focus on narratives, especially personal histories, as the medium of our study. This choice was made partly out of convenience, as a way of talking about less than everything at once. At the same time there is some motivation behind our choice of narrative.

Goffman (1974) has pointed out the replayed nature of everyday conversation. He pointed to the little narratives with which we constantly characterize ourselves and the world about us so that our listeners will be encouraged to take our view of things. Narrative for Goffman is the way we put together our reality in conversational interaction.

Halliday (1976a) and Scollon (1976) have argued for the centrality of narrative in the child's development of communicative ability. The little stories the child is encouraged to tell prepare the way for the social construction of reality observed by Goffman. Hymes (1975) has argued that narrative is the central function of language, even if it is only belatedly being recognized as such.

More recently Cazden and Hymes (1978) have brought the discussion of narrative closer to our concerns here. They have argued that within American education there is a widespread bias against the use of narrative as a communicative medium. They suggested that this bias against narrative may in fact constitute the basis for discrimination against some groups or individuals for whom narrative is a central component of communicative style. They further suggested that this bias places limits on our own ability to find adequate means of expression in the academic and educational world.

ATHABASKAN ORAL NARRATIVE

It scarcely needs to be documented that narrative is a highly significant genre in both literate and non-literate societies. The ethnographic literature as well as the history of European literature reiterate this centrality of oral narratives. We will be looking closely at oral narrative in Athabaskan society in this study as an example of the importance of narrative in the expression of communicative style. This example is critical for two reasons.

First, the patterns of interaction in Athabaskan oral narrative are very interesting in and of themselves. It has been the unfortunate tendency of some to regard Athabaskans, at least in the north, as being without highly developed art and ritual forms. We suggest that the subtlety and balance of the interactive Athabaskan oral narrative constitute an art of the highest development. It is to be admired that Athabaskans have invested the best of their artistic energies in the education of children, the management of their social relations and the entertainment of their elders through the performance of oral narratives.

Second, the potential for discrimination against minority ethnic groups is abundant throughout the interior of Alaska and northern Canada. These areas have been regularly "under-serviced" by educational, legal, and economic development agencies. This under-service is itself an expression of a profound lack of understanding of communicative style among those involved in these services. December 1991 is the date of the termination of the interim and transitional period mandated by the Alaska Native Claims Settlement Act. As this date draws closer the communicative crisis looms larger. The Athabaskan presence on lands that are highly desirable to non-Athabaskan economic and governmental interests means that the very slow progress toward Athabaskan self-determination threatens problems of a severity not yet encountered in the north. Thus while we hope in this study to make some contribution toward a future of improved communication in all interethnic contexts, we are particularly concerned with those contexts involving northern Athabaskans and other Alaska native groups.

RESEARCH ON ATHABASKAN COMMUNICATION

During the past ten years we have been involved in various aspects of this study. We have relied on a range of "data" from personal contacts throughout Alaska and northern Canada to formal ethnographic and linguistic elicitation. As contexts of interethnic communication these latter elicitations have been valuable as sources of insights. Our primary linguistic work has involved Chipewyan in Canada, and in Alaska Tanacross, Kutchin, and Koyukon. In our work as consultants to school districts and other educational, medical, legal, and planning institutions we have had the opportunity to gain insights, test hypotheses, and gather new insights in most regions of Alaska and the Yukon, as well as northern Alberta. We have observed all age groups, including young children.

It may be useful here to mention several difficulties in managing research in Athabaskan–English interethnic communication. The first of these relates to the very different views of interpersonal relationships taken by the two groups. Athabaskans offer and expect in return a high degree of respect for a person's individuality, his right to be independent, autonomous, and different from others. Our work has been guided by the assumption that it is possible to make general statements about human individuals as members of groups. This assumption, while made as well by Athabaskans, comes dangerously close to interfering with individual rights. Therefore, in conducting our research as well as in reporting on it, we have tried not to lose sight of the importance of respect for individuals. As a result, it becomes a breach of respect to specify individuals, research sites, and periods of research in a way that would single out any particular person as the source of a particular observation or generalization, especially, as we will see below, in a medium as distanced and "positively polite" as a book such as this.

A second problem has to do with the study of socialization of children. As we will argue, Athabaskans often feel that it is dangerous to the spiritual, mental, and psychological wellbeing of a child to seek to stimulate him into performance in public contexts or even to observe his behavior in any way that might intervene in his activities. As we have a commitment to respect Athabaskan views of the treatment of children it becomes, again, difficult to make closely- and publicly-documented observations without a violation of trust. It would further be an embarrassment to identify the individual children who have been observed. This then will account for the quite different treatments in our chapters four and six where we discuss different patterns of socialization.

The third problem relates to our commitment to produce research results of relevance to the communities in which the research is accomplished. Many of our "official" activities involve conducting workshops on interethnic communication, consultation on language planning, and linguistic and discourse research toward the production of orthographies, dictionaries, grammars, and publishable texts for bilingual education and other such uses. While this on the one hand limits the scope of our observations, it presents the immediate necessity to test ideas as they develop. Our continued participation in these activities critically depends on our being able to be of use. The "research" reported here amounts then to a culling from this "applied" experience of a core of central considerations that have allowed us to make sense of our daily round of interethnic communication. The test of its generalizability as research findings is our own feeling that it is making sense of communication and, we hope, the confirmation of that making sense by our readers.

DISCOURSE, FACE, AND SYSTEM

Section two presents the main body of description with which we will deal in this book. Chapter two outlines the properties of Athabaskan–English interethnic communication. We make the argument in that chapter that problems of miscommunication are based on differences in the organization of discourse. As a general description, we have attempted to keep chapter two relatively free of social-scientific jargon and have subdued our referencing of the literature in order to present at least this one chapter in a style that is more accessible to non-technical readers.

Chapter three argues that literacy as it is practiced in European-based education is intimately related to the reality set or world-view that we call the modern consciousness. This reality set is consonant with the discourse patterns discussed in chapter two. We argue that as a result, literacy in this style may be experienced by Athabaskans as interethnic communication. This may produce some of the same problems of miscommunication that we discussed in chapter two.

We outline a case of socialization to the patterns of essayist literacy, or the modern consciousness in the fourth chapter. It is our argument that these patterns are not the automatic outcome of maturation but rather are carefully inculcated through processes of socialization.

The fifth chapter turns to the set of discourse patterns and the reality set we call the bush consciousness. This set of discourse patterns is typified in our discussion of Athabaskan narrative. Our central point is that the structure of the narrative genre is not an *a priori* structure but rather is the result of face-to-face interaction between the narrator and his audience.

We then parallel chapter four with a discussion in chapter six of how children are socialized into the bush consciousness reality set and the discourse patterns typified in Athabaskan narrative. Again, it is our goal to argue that these patterns are not the simple result of maturation, nor of the absence of literacy. They are the result of the socialization to a particular set of cultural values that are the basis of an individual's identity.

The third section of the book turns to a consideration of the problem of face. In chapter seven we argue that face, or the whole

9

range of politeness phenomena, is the basis of the discourse patterns described in section two. We extend the argument of chapter five, that the discourse patterns of narrative are in fact patterns of social interaction, to argue that all discourse patterns embody expressions of face. Our point is that the differences between Athabaskan and English speakers are not simply matters of group difference but are founded on universals of human face-to-face interaction.

This consideration of face leads us in chapter eight to question the origin of group values that produce differences in face relations. If all humans given certain conditions and expectations would behave in the same way, how do certain groups tend to prefer certain conditions and to have certain expectations? Our answer is that the relationship between the universals of human interaction and particular groups is complex. To some extent values are given by history or by individual human differences. Nevertheless, the role of socialization in creating these values is central. This central role of socialization closes an internal feedback loop by which the system of discourse patterns, face values, and socialization tends to reinforce itself. Systems tend toward stability and resistance to change because of this circularity. We define interethnic communication then as communication between such systems, and from that we derive the conclusion that change cannot be introduced by unilateral decisions. Change also cannot be introduced as focused on any single element of the system. We conclude that the only viable solution to miscommunication in interethnic communication is to cultivate a deep respect for the fundamental differences of individuals, groups, and communicative styles. Cultural and ethnic pluralism must be fostered as the only solution to diversity. It is our belief that such diversity with respect is, in fact, the only means of ensuring stability in national and world communicative systems.

Two

Athabaskan-English Interethnic Communication

INTERETHNIC COMMUNICATION

Communications between members of different ethnic groups in Alaska and northern Canada, as elsewhere, frequently results in confusion, misunderstanding and conflict. This situation is not new, but in recent years is becoming aggravated by the increased amount of intrusion into every aspect of life of the bureaucratic and technological systems of modern western society. Legal and economic pressures have made many individuals feel that it is necessary in pursuit of their own best interests for them to engage in communication with members of other ethnic groups. This interethnic communication is between members of the dominant, English-speaking, western American and Canadian society and members of native groups in most cases. The confusion and misunderstanding that often results from this interethnic communication is a source of frustration for native people who feel that their legitimate and urgent needs are being ignored or misunderstood. This miscommunication is also a source of frustration for members of the dominant English-speaking society who feel they are unable to make their own points of view clear as well as being unable to understand native points of view. As miscommunication increases, racial and ethnic stereotyping begin to develop and impede further communication.

11

Recently we have begun to see that the main problem in inter-ethnic communication is not caused by grammar (Gumperz 1977a, 1977b, Gumperz & Roberts 1978). Although languages use grammar as the system of expressing ideas, in interethnic communication it is the discourse system which produces the greatest difficulty. It is the way ideas are put together into an argument, the way some ideas are selected for special emphasis, or the way emotional information about the ideas is presented that causes miscommunication. The grammatical system gives the message while the discourse system tells how to interpret the message. The greatest cause of interethnic problems lies in the area of understanding not *what* someone says but *why* he is saying it. This information about *why* people are speaking is not signaled in the same way in all ethnic groups, and so some misunderstandings can result even where the grammatical systems are nearly identical. By the same token, even where grammatical systems are quite different, communication can succeed if there is agreement about the discourse system.

We will be looking at some of the linguistic sources of inter-ethnic conflict in this chapter. First of all, the discourse system a speaker uses is learned very early in life (Scollon 1976, Halliday 1976a,b,c); probably much of it is learned before the child speaks any words. This system is learned through a long and highly involved process of socialization and communication with caregivers. It is unconscious and affects all communication in language. This discourse system is closely tied to an individual's concept of identity. Any change in the discourse system is likely to be felt as a change in personality and culture. We will describe in this chapter how inter-ethnic communication works in order to provide a basis for our later discussion of face and the interpersonal grounds on which facework is founded.

Athabaskan-English

We will only talk about communication between Athabaskans and speakers of English in this chapter and indeed throughout the book. There are no good terms to refer to the two groups of which we are speaking. By "Athabaskan" we mean anyone who has been socialized to a set of communicative patterns which have their roots in the Athabaskan languages. These people are ethnically Athabaskan on the whole but may not speak any Athabaskan language. We mean by "speakers of English" anyone whose communicative patterns are those of the dominant, mainstream American and Ca nadian English-speaking population. We know this is awkward since most of the communication we are looking at takes place in English. It seems better than using a term such as Standard English, which seems to suggest that one variety of English is to be preferred over another. Although we realize that there are many individual differences among people, we still feel that the patterns we are describing here hold true in a general way and are the patterns on which people have developed ethnic stereotypes. Because of the consistency of these ethnic stereotypes we feel there is a consistent pattern of discourse underlying this stereotyping.

FOUR AREAS OF DISCOURSE STUDY

This chapter is organized around four topics: the presentation of self, the distribution of talk, information structure, and content organization. Talking is one of the main ways in which we present ourselves to other people in the world. It is our chance to give our side of the story, to show ourselves in a particular light, to put in certain details and leave out others so that others will take our view of things. Goffman (1959, 1974) has called this aspect of communication the presentation of self. Here we will look at how differently Athabaskans and English speakers view the presentation of self and how this leads to misinterpretation.

When people talk, they have to agree on who gets to speak first, how they exchange turns and how they interrupt. One of the main areas in which interethnic communication runs into problems is when people have different ways of beginning and ending a conversation or when people have different ways of getting the floor. We call these problems the distribution of talk.

The third area we will look at is how talk makes sense. When someone is speaking and we understand the system, we can tell when he is going to go on or when he is going to quit. We can tell when he has made a statement or asked a question. We can tell what parts of his ideas he is emphasizing and what parts he is excited about. The information structuring system is what tells us these things. One reason there is difficulty in communication is that in some discourse systems information structuring is done with prosody, while in others prosody is less important. That is, in some cases it is the pitch or loudness or tone of voice that indicates information structure, while in other cases this is done with words or morphemes and with little or no change of prosody. In interethnic communication where these systems are different there is often confusion in the information structure.

Finally, we will look at what is actually said. Even here there are often disagreements about how much you should actually say and how much your listener should be able to figure out. If too much is said the listener may feel it is rude. If too little is said the listener may feel the speaker is vague or doesn't understand what he or she is talking about. The organization of the contents of talk is the fourth area we will look at.

THE PRESENTATION OF SELF

Even though we talk for many reasons, one of the main things we do when we talk is to present a view of ourselves to the listener, and of course when the listener takes a turn at speaking he either confirms or questions our view at the same time as he presents a view of himself. This presentation of self is done in many ways. It is reflected in our choice of words, in our tone of voice, in the attitudes we display and in the topics about which we talk. In talking, each participant presents a particular view of the world and the self, and as the conversation progresses these views become altered and affected by the views of the other participants. Goffman (1974, 1976) calls this changing of views the negotiation of intersubjective reality. That is, the subjective reality of each participant in a conversation is checked out against the reality of each other participant as an ongoing negotiation through which we create a social world.

Taciturnity and Volubility

One of the first observations people make about Athabaskan–English conversations, especially when these conversations are between strangers, is that Athabaskans do not talk as much as English speakers. From the Athabaskan point of view what is usually experienced is that English speakers talk all the time, or talk too much. From the English point of view Athabaskans are said not to like to talk, or to be silent. Basso (1970) has said that Apaches (southern Athabaskans) are silent in situations where the participants are unsure of how they stand with each other. That is, it is probably not right to say that Athabaskans do or do not speak less than English speakers. It seems better to focus on situations in which one group has a preference for not speaking or being taciturn.

In our own work (Scollon & Scollon 1979) we have suggested that there is a real difference between Athabaskans and English speakers in how much they choose to speak, and that this difference has to do with the negotiation of intersubjective reality. Athabaskans have a very high degree of respect for the individuality of others and a careful guarding of one's own individuality. As a result, any conversation can be threatening because of the possibility of a negotiated change of point of view. Athabaskans avoid conversation except when the point of view of all participants is well known.

On the other hand, English speakers feel that the main way to get to know the point of view of people is through conversation with them. Cocktail parties among strangers or near strangers are probably the best example of the use of conversation by English speakers to seek out acquaintance and agreement.

These ideas lead us to see that if two people who are not well known to each other meet, the English speaker will want to talk so that they can get to know each other, but the Athabaskan will want to wait until they get to know each other before feeling it would be very easy to talk. These are the situations in which the English speaker feels the Athabaskan is unusually taciturn or reserved in speaking and the Athabaskan feels that the English speaker is too talkative.

Taking the other extreme, where the participants are well known to each other, we can find Athabaskans to be very talkative. At the same time, for English speakers, the situations of longstanding personal knowledge are among the few in which it is appropriate not to talk. It is in a way a sign of intimacy for an English speaker that talk is not needed.

We can see that a very basic difference between Athabaskans and English speakers has to do with taciturnity and volubility, and this relates to the presentation of self. For English speakers, volubility is related to social distance and taciturnity to intimacy. For Athabaskans the relationship is the reverse, with volubility possible only in contexts of intimacy where there is no threat to the speaker's view of himself or the world. Since by far the greatest number of contacts between Athabaskans and English speakers happen in semi-formal business, medical, legal, or educational contexts, it is not surprising that the English preference is for a lot of talking and the Athabaskan preference is for a reserved amount of talking. This can lead to the ethnic stereotyping mentioned above. English speakers come away from the situation saying that Athabaskans do not want to talk. Athabaskans come away feeling that English speakers talk all the time. The disagreement is a very fundamental one about the presentation of self. Athabaskans prefer to show a deep respect for the individuality of others, even if this produces a difficulty in getting to know them. English speakers prefer developing contacts widely with strangers and non-intimates, even if this produces a constant state of change in the concept of self. Interethnic communication threatens a shift in these basic premises, not for the English speaker, but for the Athabaskan. Thus we can begin to see that interethnic communication in and of itself constitutes a danger to the Athabaskan. Taciturnity in the face of this danger is a viable response.

Social Relations of Dominance

Another issue in the presentation of self has to do with the power relationships between speakers. We present a different "face" to our children, to our husbands and wives, and to our parents. If the relationship between two people is one of dominance and submission, that is, if one is in a more powerful position than the other, the way one speaks will depend very much on which position he is in. The difficulty that we want to look at here is that there are several dimensions to power relationships, and Athabaskans and English speakers do not agree on how they are related.

The three relationships we want to look at are dominance, display, and dependence. Each of these has two possibilities— superordinate and subordinate for dominance, spectatorship and exhibitionism for display, and caregiving and petitioning for dependence. Bateson (1972) and Mead (1977) have said that these are different for British and Americans. Canadians appear to share many of the properties of British English speakers, and in doing so contrast with Americans. English-speaking Canadians may be said to find interethnic communication with Athabaskans somewhat less problematical in this respect. To highlight areas of potential difficulty we will talk primarily about Americans here as the extreme case when we speak of English speakers.

For American English speakers, the person in the superordinate or dominant position is the spectator and the subordinate person is the exhibitionist. What that means is that the parent as a spectator expects to watch what a child does. The child should show off his abilities to the parents and is often expected to be entertaining. In school English speakers expect children to display their abilities as exhibitionists to the teacher as spectator. There is no doubt at the same time that the teacher is in the dominant or superordinate position. To use Bateson and Mead's term, for English speakers (in America) the superordinate role is "linked" with spectatorship and the subordinate role is "linked" with exhibitionism.

This is different for Athabaskans. Children are not expected to show off for adults. Adults as either parents or teachers are supposed to display abilities and qualities for the child to learn. The adult or superordinate is in the exhibitionist role while the child is in the spectator role.

It is not difficult to see how this different linkage of dominance and display can cause confusion in any interethnic communication between nonequals. If the English speaker is the teacher and the Athabaskan is the child, then the teacher expects to be in charge, to be in the dominant role, but at the same time expects the child to display his abilities. The child, on the other hand, either expects the teacher to be the exhibitionist while he is the spectator, or if the child becomes the exhibitionist, he expects to be treated as the dominant member of the pair.

For the English-speaking teacher an Athabaskan child will either seem unduly reserved because he is spectating, or unduly aggressive if the child has assumed the superordinate role that he feels is consistent with display or exhibitionism. For the Athabaskan child the teacher will seem either incompetent because he is not exhibiting his abilities, or unduly bossy because in spite of not exhibiting he is taking the superordinate role.

These same relationships exist in other situations as well. Wherever the two participants are of unequal status this problem with the difference in linkage between dominance and display will show up. If we look back at what we said about taciturnity and volubility we can see that taciturnity is related to spectatorship and volubility to exhibitionism. What this means is that from the English speaker's point of view the person in the subordinate role, the exhibitionist, should do a lot of speaking, especially in presentting the self. The Athabaskan point of view is that the person in the superordinate role should do most of the speaking, again as the exhibitionist. So if the English speaker does most of the speaking in interethnic communication with the Athabaskan, he must interpret the Athabaskan taciturnity as displaying superiority. It is not surprising to see conflict in a situation where each speaker believes the other to be displaying a superior attitude, but this is a natural reaction to this difference in the linkage of dominance and display in nonequal social relations. As each speaker tries to take a position of subordination to the other, he unknowingly is communicating just the opposite in the other speaker's system.

The third dimension is that of dependence. In the Athabaskan system, the person in the superordinate role is assumed to have the responsibility for taking care of the one in the subordinate role. In fact, traditionally it was this dimension that gave one a position of dominance. The person who provided for others was given the dominant position as well as the right to direct others' behavior. Others were in a position of dependence and could expect the dominant person to take care of them. Basically all that was required was to make the need known for support to be given.

In the English system there is no very strong relation between dominance and dependence except between parents and children. There is little expectation that a wealthy or powerful person should distribute his wealth or power to others with less. There is even less expectation that the way to achieve power or dominance is by taking care of other people by distributing one's wealth or goods.

The result of this difference in conversation is that for Athabaskans, being in the superordinate role is related to being in the position to grant assistance to the one in the subordinate role. This produces very different assumptions about what should happen in such petitioning situations as counseling, job interviews, or welfare interviews, where the petitioner is in a dependent role. The Athabaskan point of view is that the counselor or interviewer is in the position of dominance and therefore should do most of the speaking as the exhibitionist and grant the good or service as the caregiver. The English speaker's point of view is that in the same situation, the person being interviewed should be the exhibitionist and display a full view of himself for evaluation through significant amounts of talking.

As a result of this difference in the linkage of dependence, dominance, and display, Athabaskans often feel that their clear rights as dependents of the American bureaucratic system have not been granted, even though they have taken the proper subordinate, petitioning position by not speaking and carefully observing the English speaker. English speakers, on the other hand, feel that Athabaskans being interviewed do not display enough of themselves for the interviewer to evaluate their need, that they have become sullen and withdrawn or perhaps even acted superior, as if they needed no help.

Prohibited Actions

The English idea of "putting your best foot forward" conflicts directly with an Athabaskan taboo. It is normal in situations of unequal status relations for English speakers in Canada as well as in America to display oneself in the best light possible. In job interviews, in school, in meeting strangers, or in getting arrested for speeding it is expected that one will display only one's best qualities, abilities, and accomplishments. One will speak highly of the future, as well. It is normal to present a career or life trajectory of success and planning.

In conversations where this presentation of self is done in face-to-face contact this display of one's accomplishments is played down only by what Pawley and Syder (n.d.) have called the "reduction principle." By this they mean that instead of showing your qualities, abilities, or opinions in the strongest light you reduce them somewhat, just by the right amount, so that the other speaker can boast for you. This is a kind of lure that is cast out in order to make your conversational partner do some of the work of displaying your abilities. You understate your case and your partner then builds it up.

One must be careful in this system neither to overstate nor to understate the view one presents of oneself. This view must be good but not so good that there will be nothing left for your partner to say on your behalf. On the other hand, too much reduction, too much playing down of your own position is heard as too big a lure. Your partner must either take your position too strongly, and thereby endanger his own position, or take your position at face value.

This English system is very different from the Athabaskan system in which it is considered inappropriate and bad luck to anticipate good luck, to display oneself in a good light, to predict the future, or to speak badly of another's luck. The concept of *injîh* as it is expressed in Tanacross Athabaskan means that if you intended to go out hunting moose you would never say so directly. The most you might say is that you are going out and you hope you will not be hungry. To speak too directly of the future prospect of a good hunt would be to court bad luck.

It would be quite inappropriate to speak of one's plans for some time later in life or in any way to indicate some expectation that one's future life will be good. Since it might be taken as suggesting having had such plans, even good references to one's past experiences are often uncomfortable for Athabaskan speakers.

It is not surprising, then, that much Athabaskan–English interethnic communication gets confused by a misinterpretation on this dimension. Especially in interviews and other gatekeeping situations the English speaker expects the Athabaskan to present himself in the best possible light. He must display his achievements of the past and his ambitions for the future if he wants the job. At the same time the Athabaskan will feel that any good presentation of himself will court bad luck and work against his prospects of getting the job. Because this self-deprecation is so strong for Athabaskans, the English speaker cannot take it as simple reduction and so takes it as the simple truth instead. Again, we have a case in which the more the Athabaskan seeks to succeed the stronger it works against him in communications with English speakers. The more the English speaker wishes to "draw out" the Athabaskan, the more embarrassing it becomes for both; these situations often end in failure.

In the reverse situation, where the Athabaskan is in the dominant position and the English speaker is in the subordinate position, the English speaker seems too boastful or too careless with his luck because of his predictions of his future and the open display of his past. Again, the result is that these communicative difficulties turn into ethnic stereotypes. The Athabaskan thinks of the English speaker as boastful or careless with luck and the future, while the

English speaker thinks of the Athabaskan as unsure of himself, withdrawn, and aimless.

The Dilemma in the Presentation of Self

The problems encountered by Athabaskans and English speakers in interethnic communication begin with the presentation of self. The English speaker seeks to display his own abilities, the best side of himself, through talking. The Athabaskan, on the other hand, avoids these self-displays. The result is a feeling that English speakers prefer to speak a lot more than Athabaskans.

Where the relationship is one of dominance and submission this problem is accentuated by a different linkage of dominance, display, and dependence. The English speaker expects the dominant person to be the quiet one, the spectator, and expects that aid will only be given where the need is clearly displayed, and, we might add, where there is a legal or strong social requirement. The Athabaskan expects the dominant person to be the main speaker, the exhibitionist, and to maintain his dominance by giving help to the ones he dominates.

The difficulties produced by these different linkages of dominance, display, and dependence are further compounded by the English speaker's assumption that one will put his best foot forward and the Athabaskan assumption that one will not speak very well of himself.

The result of these communication problems is that each group then ethnically stereotypes the other. The English speaker comes to believe that the Athabaskan is unsure, aimless, incompetent, and withdrawn. The Athabaskan comes to believe that the English speaker is boastful of his own abilities, sure he can predict the future, careless with luck, and far too talkative.

These ethnic stereotypes are widely believed to be true because each encounter, especially under stressful conditions, tends to replicate the last and produces more deeply entrenched attitudes. It is important to see that from the Athabaskan point of view, the English speaker is not really as sure of himself and as cocky about the future as he seems. From the English point of view, the Athabaskan is not as aimless and unsure as he appears to be. These stereotyped views are the result of very predictable factors relating to the cultural expectations of the two groups. The two groups have very different views of the purpose of talking and how their goals should be accomplished through talk. These different views are closely related to structural features of the discourse. These features are the means by which we display the attitudes and expectations we have discussed here as the presentation of self. As we will begin to show in the following three sections, these structural factors can be isolated and analyzed. We feel that by undertaking this analytical study of the discourse factors governing interethnic communication we can move toward loosening some of the stereotyped ethnic attitudes that we have discussed.

THE DISTRIBUTION OF TALK

When two or more people talk together, it takes a lot of coordination to keep things going smoothly. Although it does not seem like it, in ordinary conversation the various speakers are careful not to talk all at once or to interrupt or to fail to answer if there is a question. This cooperation takes a good bit of work and common understanding. In interethnic communication there are often differences in the systems of the speakers, so that mistakes happen that lead to further misunderstandings. We will look in this section at how conversationalists decide who speaks first, how topics are controlled, how turns at talking are exchanged, and how conversations are ended.

Who Speaks First

When an Athabaskan and a speaker of English talk to each other, it is very likely that the English speaker will speak first. Many people have observed this. It is not hard to see why the English speaker will speak first if we consider what was said about the presentation of self. The Athabaskan will feel it is important to know the relationship between the two speakers before speaking. The English speaker will feel talking is the best way to establish a relationship. While the Athabaskan is waiting to see what will happen between them, the English speaker will begin speaking, usually asking questions in fact, to find out what will happen. Only where there is a longstanding relationship and a deep understanding between the two speakers is it likely that the Athabaskan will initiate the conversation.

Control of Topic

It might not seem very important at first glance who speaks first in a conversation. Studies of conversation have shown, however, that the person who speaks first also controls the topic of conversation. Schegloff (1972) found that the person who spoke first took the role of the summoner. His speech in effect asks the other speaker for the right to talk. The second speaker answers but in a very open way. The answer of the second speaker gives the first speaker the right to go ahead and talk. The first speaker then introduces the topic of the conversation to which the second must then reply. If the second speaker wants to introduce his own topic he must wait for a chance to introduce it later, after they have talked about the first speaker's topic.

These general rules seem so obvious and trivial that it is hard to believe how strictly we hold to them. It is easy to see how strong these rules are, though, by trying to break them. If someone calls on the phone (the phone ring is the first speaker), and if you answer by talking about what you want to talk about, both you and the caller will feel something very strange has happened. During their study, one of Schegloff's colleagues was being troubled by obscene phone calls. She found that if she picked up the phone but did not say anything, the caller would not go on to say any obscenities. He was following the conversational rules that would only allow him to speak after the second speaker answered. He followed conversational rules even though he was violating the moral rules of the same society.

In another study Scollon (1976) found that a one year old child learned these conversational rules before she was two years old. A one year old has very little she can say easily. The child in that study, Brenda, found that if she was the first speaker she could talk about what she wanted to talk about. She used one word, "here," as a summons. She would give a piece of paper or trash or almost anything to someone else and say "here." The other person would take it and say "thank you." Then Brenda would say whatever she wanted to say.

Sometimes an adult would try to speak to Brenda first. She would refuse to answer. If the adult persisted she would say "here" and hand him something. That would make her the first speaker and ultimately give her the right to introduce her topic. Brenda had learned how to use speaking first to keep control of the topic of conversation by the time she was two year old.

We have said that in Athabaskan–English conversations the English speaker almost always speaks first. This has the consequence of allowing him to introduce his own topic and of making it very difficult for the Athabaskan to introduce any other topic. The general result of these two facts is that in interethnic communications between Athabaskans and English speakers the topic of conversation is almost always the English speaker's topic, not the Athabaskan's.

Another complication is introduced by the fact that at least some Athabaskans use a conversational greeting that gives the answerer the right to introduce the topic. At Fort Chipewyan, Alberta, it is common to greet people with ʔɛdlánɨðen "what are you thinking?" The appropriate response is an open-ended introduction of the answerer's topic if he should choose to say something.

Here as before these discourse problems lead to stereotyping. The Athabaskan starts to feel that his ideas are always being ignored. At the same time he feels that the English speaker is either egocentric or ethnocentric. He feels that the English speaker only wants to talk about his own ideas. From the English speaker's point of view it seems either that the Athabaskan does not have any ideas of his own or that when they are introduced these ideas are off the topic. By putting together the assumptions about the presentation of self that Athabaskans and English speakers hold and a quite mechanical rule of conversational interchange, we get a situation in which one speaker is always in control of what the participants talk about.

The Exchange of Speaking Turns

We have said that at least in English conversation one speaker begins, a second answers, the first introduces the topic, and the second continues on that topic. Of course, conversations can be more complicated than that. There may be more than two speakers, for one thing. But to keep this discussion from getting too complex, we will just talk about two-person conversation.

As the conversation goes on the speakers continue to take turns in speaking. They do not normally both speak at the same time. In fact, simultaneous speech is usually a good sign that something has gone wrong. When the timing goes off so far that both speakers start speaking together it usually takes some time to smooth things out again. Usually after one speaker finishes the other can take a turn. If the other one does not say anything, then the first speaker can take another turn if he wishes. If the other comes in too soon it feels as if he is interrupting.

Problems start to come up when two speakers have different systems for pausing between turns. Generally speaking, Athabaskans allow a slightly longer pause between sentences than do English speakers. The difference is probably not more than half a second in length, but it has an important effect on interethnic communication. When an English speaker pauses he waits for the regular length of time (around one second or less), that is, *his* regular length of time, and if the Athabaskan does not say anything, the English speaker feels he is free to go on and say anything else he likes. At the same time the Athabaskan has been waiting his regular length of time before coming in. He does not want to interrupt the English speaker. This length of time we think is around one and one-half seconds. It is just enough longer that by the time the Athabaskan is ready to speak the English speaker is already speaking again. So the Athabaskan waits again for the next pause. Again, the English speaker begins just enough before the Athabaskan was going to speak. The net result is that the Athabaskan can never get a word in edgewise (an apt metaphor in this case), while the English speaker goes on and on.

The Athabaskan point of view is that it is difficult to make one's whole point. The length of pause that the Athabaskan takes while expecting to continue is just about the length of pause the English speaker takes in exchanging turns. If an Athabaskan has in mind a series of sentences to say, it is most likely that at the end of the first one the English speaker will think that he has finished because of the length of the pause and will begin speaking. The Athabaskan feels he has been interrupted and the English speaker feels the Athabaskan never makes sense, never says a whole coherent idea. Much of this misunderstanding is the result of something like a one-half second difference in the timing of conversational pauses, but it can result in strong stereotypical responses to the opposite ethnic group.

A second factor in the exchange of speaking turns that only increases the difficulty we are looking at here is that there are different expectations about how long a speaker should be allowed to speak at one turn. Generally Athabaskans expect that a speaker will take as long as necessary to develop an idea. The ideal situation is that of an older speaker, a person in a clear superordinate position, narrating a traditional story. Although this ideal may not often be practiced, there is nevertheless an expectation that something like a monologue is the normal speaking turn. The role of other speakers is that of an audience that by frequent traffic signal responses indicates that it is following. English speakers, on the other hand, treat monologues as exceptions, with the norm being the dialogue in which speakers exchange more or less equal turns.

In Athabaskan–English interethnic communication, the expectation that English speakers have is rarely fulfilled. True dialogue rarely occurs. The reason for this has been given. The exchange of turns works toward the English speaker's continually regaining the floor and against the Athabaskan's being able to hold the floor for more than brief speaking turn. Where an Athabaskan may expect to get his turn after a long English monologue he rarely gets more than a brief statement before another English monologue begins. The result is again stereotyping of the English speaker as egocentric and the Athabaskan as having no ideas of his own.

Departure Formulas

It is safe to say that an Athabaskan–English conversation will usually begin with the English speaker speaking first. It is almost as certain that it will end with the Athabaskan making no formal close. On the surface the explanation seems simple enough. Most of the formulas for ending conversation refer to the future. As we have said, Athabaskans feel it is bad luck to make predictions about the future. This applies even to such routine statements as "I'll see you later" or "I'll see you tomorrow." Where the English speakers feel these are simple closing statements, ways of saying "Now our talk is ended," they carry an overtone of bad luck for the Athabaskan and thus are avoided.

The impression of these closing formulas from the Athabaskan point of view again confirms the English speaker's bravado regarding his good luck and future. From the English speaker's point of view, the lack of closings gives a feeling that something has gone wrong in the communication. As we have reason to believe now, that is very likely to be true; but it may be misleading. The conversation may have been very compatible and yet leave the English speaker feeling that something went wrong because of the lack of a close.

We need to look a bit closer at departures to understand this problem. As Goffman (1974) has said, departures do much more than bring a conversation to a close. They set up the conditions for future conversations. English speakers feel it is essential at the end of each encounter to be clear just where you stand with the other speaker. The closing formula is the way this is done. Something as simple as "It's been nice talking to you" suggests that you expect to do more of it in the future. As we depart we prepare the future, and it is this aspect of the formula that for the English speaker fits in well with the general negotiation of intersubjective reality. The departure is the final check on where you have gotten to in the negotiation that has taken place. It cements this into place so that the negotiation can be resumed at the next opportunity.

This preparation of the future through the departure formula is directly contrary to the Athabaskan prohibition on speaking strongly of the future. If one enjoyed a conversation, it would be bad luck indeed to say so and that you hoped it would happen again. So in closing a conversation as in beginning it, the Athabaskan is careful not to display carelessness or to present himself in too favorable a light. The English speaker who has begun the conversation as a way of getting to know the other closes the conversation with an indirect but important summary of how things have gone. Perhaps the worst outcome from the English point of view is a complete rupture of the relationship. This would be shown by a violation of discourse conventions, including the convention of a formulated departure. The Athabaskan, being careful of courting bad luck, may quite unknowingly signal to the English speaker the worst possibility, that there is no hope of getting together again to speak.

The Importance of Discourse and Cultural Factors

In interethnic communication between English speakers and Athabaskans, talk is distributed so that the English speaker is favored as first speaker, as controller of topic, as principal speaker, and yet in the end he may not have any conclusive idea of what went on. For the Athabaskan speaker it is difficult to get the floor, to bring the conversation around to his own topic, and in the end to feel he has had much effect on the outcome. This situation is prepared by cultural expectations about the presentation of self. It works through the mechanics of a slight difference in pausing systems and the general mechanics of turn taking in human communication. The result is a considerable potential for difficulty in interethnic communication. It is important to point out now that we have not yet mentioned any factors that have to do with the grammatical or lexical structure of language directly. The potential difficulties and misunderstandings that we have discussed are the same whether the communication is carried on in English, Athabaskan, so-called Village English, or any combination of these. As long as the discourse patterns and the presentation of self are clearly Athabaskan in origin on the one hand and English in origin on the other these possibilities of problems will arise.

At first it will seem ironic that the situation in which there is the greatest potential for problems is where the language being used by the two speakers is the most similar. We are so accustomed to thinking that communication is a matter of grammar and vocabulary that if the grammar and vocabulary are the same or similar for two speakers it is difficult to believe that there might be trouble. Yet, as we have said earlier, these discourse patterns and cultural expectations are learned very early in life and change slowly. Even where someone learns to speak a new language later in life, it is very likely that he will speak it using the discourse patterns of his early language training. In present-day Alaska and Canada, many people who do not speak any Athabaskan language have nevertheless learned Athabaskan discourse patterns which are essential for effective communication within the village, even though the language used may be English. We want to be careful then not to think that understanding will be automatic just because two speakers do not differ greatly in grammar or vocabulary. Assumptions about the presentation of self and the distribution of talk in interethnic communication lie at the bottom of many communicative conflicts.

INFORMATION STRUCTURE

We now want to look at some of the ways information is signaled in Athabaskan and English. When we say information we do not mean the basic idea being expressed. What we mean is information about how the listener is supposed to interpret that idea. The basic idea in spoken English on the whole is expressed by the words and the grammar and the information structure is expressed by the intonation and stress. We will use the word *prosody* to cover intonation, stress, tone of voice, and other non-grammatical elements of the message.

As an example of information structure, if I say, "I saw a moose standing there," it means one thing. If I say "I saw a *moose* standing there," and stress the word "moose," it means something else. When I stress "moose" by saying it a little louder and higher in pitch, the sentence means that I saw a moose but I expected to see something else, or nothing at all. The stress means I not only saw the moose, but I was surprised by it. There are two messages here. The primary one is about seeing the moose and it is expressed by the sentence in its plain form. The secondary message is that I was surprised. That message is expressed by prosody, in this case with stress. When we say "information structure," then, we mean the messages about the message that are expressed by such things as the prosody in English.

Prosody and Morphemes

In English the information structure is normally shown by the prosody. You can tell how to interpret the main message by paying attention to the stress, intonation, or tone of voice. In Athabaskan, though, the information structure is often expressed by morphemes rather than by prosody. These are normally suffixes or words at the beginning or the end of a phrase that tell you how to interpret the whole phrase. As an example, a man was telling a story in Chipewyan about a beaver hunt. On his way home he came across a bear in the trail. Of course he was surprised by it, and in Chipewyan he said sas náðer k'ɛ́ sas means "bear", náðer means "it was standing there," and k'ɛ́ does not really have any meaning of its own. It means the same thing as the stress on *moose* when I said, "I saw a *moose* standing there." The morpheme k'ɛ́ means he was surprised. The meaning of this morpheme is that the phrase is to be emphasized. It tells you something about the information structure, not the basic idea of seeing the bear.

We have used this example to show how Athabaskan uses a morpheme with no change in the stress to show the information structure, but English uses stress without any additional morphemes. This can cause confusion in two ways. When someone who speaks English tries to learn Athabaskan, he has a tendency to try to use stress to mark information structure instead of emphatic morphemes and the like. On the other hand, when an Athabaskan learns English, he has a tendency to make mistakes with stress and other prosodic marking of information structure. The result is the same in both directions. It is difficult for listeners to follow what is being said. You can understand *what* a person says but not *why* he said it or what his attitude toward it was. These *why's* are absolutely essential for making sense in conversation.

Another morpheme that is very important in Chipewyan is the morpheme ʔɛkú· or kú· (Scollon 1977, Scollon & Scollon 1979). If it is translated it means "and then" but more often than not it does not literally mean "and then." It is used much more as a way of signaling information structure. The main function we found in stories was to set off main sections of the story. It is much like the indentation we use for paragraphs in written English. Athabaskan languages all have some morpheme that functions like kú·, and as a result when Athabaskans learn English they often feel a need for a morpheme to signal the episodic structure of a story. Most often the choice is *and* or *and then*. These sound like hesitations or indicators of insecurity to an English speaker. When we have analyzed stories told by Athabaskans in English, however, we have found that *and* (or *and um*) is used as a very formal marker of the plot and episodic structure.

This can of course cause difficulty in interethnic communication. Where the Athabaskan is careful in speaking English to show the formal structure of the story, the English speaker hears it as halting and unsure. At the same time the English use of prosody to mark episodic structure may not be perceived at all by the Athabaskan who is expecting morphemes as formal markers. The English narrative may sound unorganized to the Athabaskan listener.

In conversational uses similar problems arise. When the morpheme kú· in Chipewyan comes between two clauses, if the first one is a subordinate clause kú· is reduced to -ú or sometimes just a high tone on the last syllable of the subordinate clause. When a Chipewyan speaker speaks in English he may raise the last syllable to show grammatical subordination. The English speaker would hear this rise in pitch as a question, and would answer. The result is that the English speaker has taken over the floor right between a subordinate clause and a main clause because of a misinterpretation of the marker of subordination. To the Athabaskan it seems like a rude interruption in the middle of a sentence. To the English speaker it sounds as if the Athabaskan does not finish his sentences.

Here we can see how the distribution of talk can become confused because of a difference in information structure. Basically the same structures are marked, but in English it is done prosodically and in Athabaskan morphologically. Attempts by English speakers and Athabaskans directly to transfer their prosodic systems or their morphological systems into the other language produce misinterpretation of the information structure which results in further problems with the general distribution of talk.

Pausing

We have mentioned pausing several times, especially in connection with the distribution of talk. The role of pausing in oral narratives is extremely important and will be discussed later in relation to grounding and perspective in narrative structure. For the moment, as a general statement we can say that pausing figures more importantly in Athabaskan information structure than in English. Pauses in Athabaskan speech are more frequent and longer than in English speech. Pauses are essential in indicating the difference between backgrounded and foregrounded information. Emphasis is largely determined by pausing. For now it is important to note that the pause is a vulnerable point in the discourse because of the problems with the distribution of talk we have discussed here. Just as the Athabaskan is emphasizing a point, the English speaker interrupts because he feels the Athabaskan is not going to go on. The result is the failure of communication and the ethnic stereotyping that follows.

On the Border of Grammar

We have suggested several ways that differences between Athabaskan and English information structuring affect interethnic communication between the groups in this section on information structure. As we have seen, the information structure relates much more closely to the grammatical structure of the English and Athabaskan languages than the presentation of self and distribution of talk that we discussed above. We are at the border of the grammar.

Earlier in this paper we said that the main problems in interethnic communication were not caused by grammar. Now we can expand that statement a bit and say that we do not see any clear connection between grammar and interethnic communication except for the obvious connection that people have to speak in the same language or at least understand each other's languages for interethnic communication to happen at all.

Athabaskan is very different from English in grammatical structure. The Athabaskan verb is complex with many prefixes, suffixes, and stem variants all contributing to quite subtle semantic distinctions. In English these distinctions, when they are made, are indicated by either the choice of the word or by the order of the words, with fairly uncomplicated prefixes and suffixes. We do not see at the time of writing this that there is any clear connection between these major differences between English and Athabaskan grammar and any problems in interethnic communication.

Village English is more often talked about in discussions of interethnic communication in Alaska and Canada. We would say the same thing about grammar in that case. In spite of differences in grammar and vocabulary between Village English and other varieties of English, we have little evidence that these differences are very important in causing problems in interethnic communication. The problems caused by differences in discourse structure certainly loom much larger in any total picture of Athabaskan–English interethnic communication. We would like to suggest a deemphasis on grammatical and vocabulary issues in understanding interethnic communication. In our research these have largely been beside the point in trying to understand communicative conflict.

CONTENT ORGANIZATION

The last problem we want to look at has to do with what is actually said and how it is conceptually organized. We have already talked about some of this under the presentation of self and can begin with the problem of explicitness.

Explicitness

We have observed that both Athabaskans and English speakers sometimes feel that the others do not "come right out and say" things. We do not want to say that either group is more explicit but that they are explicit in different ways or at different times. This is what causes the confusion.

We have already looked at one example. Athabaskans feel uncomfortable about presenting themselves in too favorable a light. This often results in not being very explicit about one's own accomplishments, abilities, or plans. The English speaker on the other hand is likely to be very explicit about such things. If we think about this we can see then why direct questions can be felt by Athabaskans to be rude. A direct question asks the answerer to be quite explicit about something. If that person has been avoiding a delicate area the question may sound like a request to boast or in general to court bad luck, and it will be evaded.

In another case we can see both explicitness and inexplicitness working. English speakers use people's names to refer to them and generally do not show respect for elders by avoiding their names. An aunt would be referred to as "Aunt Jessie" without any feeling of disrespect, and it would be clear to which aunt the speaker was referring. An Athabaskan in the same situation would prefer not to mention the aunt by name but would rather use the Athabaskan term meaning perhaps "my father's sister" or an English translation. This would be fully explicit in most cases and identify the right person without showing disrespect by using a personal name. Yet this explicit reference is heard by the English speaker as evasive or unnecessarily inexplicit.

Conceptual Organization, Threes and Fours

For some time folklorists have known that European folktales are organized around themes of three parts. We have "Goldilocks and the Three Bears;" if a character has to go through ordeals there are usually three of them; if a king has daughters he has three, and they marry three brothers; and so on. We have only really noticed recently that this organization around threes is more than just folklore. The September 1978 (Vol. 80, no. 3) issue of *American An-*

thropologist is a good example of "three bears" organization. On the cover the key papers are listed as follows:

> The Veil of Objectivity: Prophecy, Divination, and Social Inquiry
>
> Sex, Status, and Authority in Egalitarian Society
> Structures, Realities, and Blind Spots

There are three papers. Each has three subsections in its title. We are not sure yet just how significant this sort of patterning is in organizing human thinking, but it is likely to be quite important.

Some time ago Toelken (1969) said that Navajo stories were organized around themes of four, not three. This would mean a potential source for confusion in interethnic communication if English speakers were organizing around threes and Athabaskans around fours.

We found in our work at Fort Chipewyan (Scollon & Scollon 1979) that when a storyteller told a story in Athabaskan it was organized around twos and fours. This organization was carefully and formally marked and regular throughout. The story had two main episodes, plus an initial and a final making four sections. Each of the main two episodes was subdivided again in units of two and four. When the same person told the same story to us in English the story was organized in groups of threes. At first we thought that it was because he had conceptually reorganized the story for the second telling. We found out, however, that this reorganization was because of our responses. We had not been able to follow the Athabaskan version and so had not interfered with his telling. We did understand the English version and all the way through said "uh huh" where we thought it was appropriate. His reorganization into different units reflects *our* responses more than his own organization. Or maybe it is better to say that in the English version the storyteller and the listeners cooperated to create a situational reorganization of the story.

We can see then how this difference in organization could produce disorganization in the discourse with the listener often responding at the wrong time from the speaker's point of view. This organization by regular units or "chunks" of three or four is probably even more important in terms of memory and cognitive processing. Kintsch (1977, Kintsch & Green 1978) has found that if you ask English-speaking college students to remember Athabaskan stories (in English) they only remember three of the four parts. Either one part is left out completely or two are combined to produce a total of three parts. The same students have no difficulty with European folktales organized around themes of threes.

Differences in Organization

This suggests that some of the conflict in Athabaskan–English interethnic communication may come from a very basic difference in themes of conceptual organization. These differences would affect ongoing communication by causing speakers always to be out of synchrony with each other. Each would often feel the other was responding at the wrong time. In longer units of talk such as stories it would give the English speaker the feeling that an Athabaskan story was always a little bit too long or had an irrelevant section. It would give the Athabaskan a feeling that an English story always left something out—the fourth part.

This difference would also affect longstanding communication patterns by producing different memory structures of communicative events. An Athabaskan and an English speaker may well remember very different things to have happened in a conversation because of different themes of organization. The result in all cases would be a feeling that the other did not make sense in some profound way, that one could just never figure out what interethnic communication had been about.

ETHNIC STEREOTYPES

We have now outlined what we see as the main issues involved in Athabaskan–English interethnic communication. Now we would like to summarize the problems in a fairly schematic way by rephrasing them from the point of view of both sides. We will defer until later our recommendations for how these patterns might be brought into better synchrony. For now we only wish to register a caution about the tentativeness of our understanding and the deep personal and social significance of change in discourse patterns.

What's Confusing

We list, in the following table, in a brief way the things that English speakers and Athabaskans find confusing in interethnic communication.

Table 1

What's confusing to English speakers about Athabaskans	What's confusing to Athabaskans about English speakers
They do not speak	They talk too much
They keep silent	They always talk first
They avoid situations of talking	They talk to strangers or people they don't know
They only want to talk to close acquaintances	They think they can predict the future
They play down their own abilities	They brag about themselves
They act as if they expect things to be given to them	They don't help people even when they can
They deny planning	They always talk about what's going to happen later
They avoid direct questions	They ask too many questions
They never start a conversation	They always interrupt
They talk off the topic	They only talk about what they are interested in
They never say anything about themselves	They don't give others a chance to talk
They are slow to take a turn in talking	They are always getting excited when they talk
They ask questions in unusual places	They aren't careful when they talk about things or people
They talk with a flat tone of voice	
They are too indirect, inexplicit	
They don't make sense	
They just leave without saying anything	

We hope that this chapter will help the reader to see why each group says and feels these things about the other group. Of course there are other things that might be added to this list. We think that the things in this list are all related to discourse processes. People feel this way because of what happens when they talk together. If there is any hope of improving interethnic communication we feel it will have to be based on understanding discourse processes.

A CAUTION ABOUT CHANGE

We have spent almost all of our space in this chapter talking about differences in discourse systems and how they may produce conflict and confusion in interethnic communication. It is because of these confusions that much ethnic stereotyping develops. While we would hope for an improvement in interethnic relations through an understanding of discourse processes we want to point out that stereotyping works in two directions. A speaker not only decides what another person is like on the basis of how he carries on in discourse; he also makes important decisions about what he himself is like from the same discourse. We believe that discourse patterns are among the strongest expressions of personal and cultural identity. To a great extent a person feels he is what he is because of the way he talks with others. Discourse patterns are very closely tied up with a person's personality and culture.

If we suggest change we have to be very aware that we are not only suggesting change in discourse patterns. We are suggesting change in a person's identity. If someone says that an English speaker should be less talkative, less self-assertive, less interested in the future, he is saying at the same time that he should become a different person. He is saying that he should identify less with his own culture and more with another. If someone says an Athabaskan should talk more about plans, should speak out more on his own opinions, or not be so indirect, he is saying that he should stop being so Athabaskan. He is saying he should change in personal identity and cultural identity.

As we write this it is impossible and undesirable for us to say what decision any person or groups should want to make about their own discourse patterns. Change is both slow and serious. That is exactly why the confusions and conflicts continue to exist. We believe it is important for all of us to know and understand just how we are communicating the stereotypes that others hold about us. We feel it is also very important for anyone engaged in language work whether teaching or research to fully understand what it means to propose changes in people's use of language. We believe that the understanding of discourse in interethnic communication is a matter of deep human importance.

PART TWO

DISCOURSE AND REALITY SET IN INTERETHNIC COMMUNICATION

THREE

THE MODERN CONSCIOUSNESS AND LITERACY

DISCOURSE, LITERACY, AND REALITY SET

Two themes currently underlie much interest and activity in interdisciplinary work involving education, anthropology, and linguistics. A strong interest has been developing in the study of discourse, especially in interethnic communication. The work of Gumperz (Gumperz & Roberts 1978, Gumperz 1977a,b) has focused on communication between ethnic groups as the most productive arena in which to gain insights into the signaling mechanisms by which speakers communicate information about messages in discourse. As we have shown in the preceding chapter, racial and ethnic stereotyping may develop in interethnic communication by inferences which relate directly to the discourse structure.

A second theme has developed around the issue of literacy. Various researchers (Scribner & Cole 1978a,b, Scribner 1979, Goody 1977, Olson 1977a,b) have begun pointing out the centrality of a particular view of reading and writing to education in America. Others (Grace in press) have shown that this view also permeates work in linguistics. We have begun to see that we have taken a particular model of prose style as the central, organizing model of our view of language. From this view have evolved a complex of theoretical and educational positions that we are now seeking to unravel.

41

A third theme we would add to this is reality set. In our work at Fort Chipewyan, Alberta (Scollon & Scollon 1979) we described a world view and orientation to learning which we called the "bush consciousness." We contrasted this reality set with the predominant Euro-Canadian and American reality set, the "modern consciousness." For this latter concept we relied on the work of Berger, Berger and Kellner (1973), who have described this as the orientation toward knowledge taken in modern bureaucratic and technological society. We have used the term "reality set" to indicate that this is a cognitive orientation toward the everyday world including the learning of that world.

We will suggest first in this chapter that the essayist prose style which we have taken as our model of literacy is to a large extent defined by discourse properties. We will then argue that these patterns are highly compatible with the modern consciousness, if not in fact an alternate phrasing of the same concept. We will then refer to our special case of interethnic discourse, Athabaskan–English interethnic communication, and suggest that because the discourse patterns of the essayist style of writing are basically the same as those of the English speaker in Athabaskan–English interethnic communication, the Athabaskan experiences literacy as an instance of Athabaskan–English interethnic communication. We suggest from this that because learning to read and write in the essayist manner is in fact learning new patterns of discourse, literacy for an Athabaskan is experienced as a change in ethnicity as well as a change in reality set. We close by explaining a known case of Athabaskan literacy as being very different structurally from essayist literacy.

VARIETIES OF LITERACY

As we work into our understanding of literacy, three areas of insight are developing: the historical, the comparative, and the developmental. In European history we now see essayist literacy as a relatively dateable phenomenon. It shares with many other developments a common orientation and a common past. At the same time when we compare European literacy with Asian literacy we see that the existence of two major orientations to the written word are not necessarily mutually exclusive within one society nor sequentially related as historical developments. Finally as we look at the development of literacy in formerly oral societies we see that there may be differential distribution of literacy styles. In order to understand literacy as a problem of interethnic communication we first need to understand some of the relevant structural differences among types of literacy.

The Enlightenment Discontinuity

Much of what we take for granted in our contemporary world came into existence around two to three hundred years ago as part of a general reorganization of European knowledge structures. In a series of books Foucault (1973, 1976, 1977a,b) has tied together the beginning of what he calls an "episteme." He sees as related the development of the modern Sing Sing-style prison after the model of Jeremy Bentham, the workhouse, the modern public school and examination system, the military review, the zoological garden and botanical garden, historical-comparative linguistics and the modern concept of literature and essayist prose. Although his argument is complex and not without internal problems, it is important to see in these developments a similar orientation to knowledge. The idea of the modern prison is the same as that of the workhouse or factory. A single observer may watch, and through watching control, the activity of a large group of people. People are arranged as entities displayed in separate cells or working positions which by their arrangement display the ordering of the·penal or productive system.

A zoo, a garden, or a military review is much the same in its orderly display to the view of the ruling mind which orders and arranges the system. The visual domain is the organizing domain. Other relationships are subordinated. The logic of relationships between species and genera on the basis of morphology is paralleled in natural history, comparative linguistics, and penal discipline. A rose is related to other plants, not to the soil in which it grows. A horse is related to mammals, not to the grasses it eats. What becomes significant in writing are the grammatical relationships internal to the text. The relationship of the text to the world of action is subordinated to its internal arrangements.

Goody (1977a) has argued that literacy leads to organization by classification through the access to display or order that the visual mode provides. The reorganization that was experienced in

Europe some two hundred or more years ago could then be seen as an historical outcome of literacy, or to be more exact, widespread literacy. Ong (1958, 1967, 1977) has argued that this new orientation to language and thought was a result of printing, which facilitated both visual display and highly accurate replication. That visual display became accessible to a much larger audience with printing.

Another important factor in the European reorganization of knowledge was the methodism of Peter Ramus (1515–1572). Ong (1958) discusses the great influence that Ramus and his followers had in organizing schooling and pedagogy in Europe around orderly "methodized" visual displays. The emphasis in schooling on organizing knowledge paralleled the view of language as part of this world of knowledge. Language came to be viewed as primarily visual, that is as writing, as highly organized or grammatical and as a transparent representation of the natural order of the universe.

Olson (1977a,b) has associated this reorientation of language toward the text with the somewhat earlier Protestant reform movements in Europe, and especially with the work of Luther. The text was supreme to Luther. Salvation was to be achieved through a deeper reading of the text, not by reference to knowledge found outside the text. He went on to compare this orientation to the explicit statements of the Royal Society of London that all text which was not clear and sufficient in its own right was to be rejected from their proceedings.

Although the reasons are not all clear, it seems now that at least by two hundred years ago, European knowledge had been reorganized in such a way that nature was taken as lawful, orderly, and independent of human activities. Language as a part of nature was taken to share these properties. At the same time language was seen as the clear reflection of the orderliness of the natural world. All instances of language that showed these properties of clarity and transparency were judged as natural. Language that was unclear, contextual, symbolic, or not strictly grammatical was judged unnatural and (by the wisdom of the Enlightenment) an offense to God's natural law. It was in this intellectual atmosphere that the English essayist prose style, which certainly had older roots, became enshrined as the natural means for the expression of truth and knowledge. It became both the medium and the ultimate goal of schooling. Access to knowledge has been seen as isomorphic with fluency in the essayist style for at least two hundred years now in Europe and it is because of this that the recent decline in this ability in public school students has been viewed with alarm. The decline in essayist literacy has been viewed as the decline of knowledge itself.

Chinese Literacy

It is striking how little Asian literacy is mentioned in general discussions of literacy. What we wish to add here is just the suggestion that this is in itself an indication of the nearly complete identification of literacy with the European essayist style.

There have been at least two strong and ancient literacy traditions in China, the Confucianist and the Buddhist. O'Harrow (1978) has argued that because of important differences in these traditions, Buddhist literacy was disseminated throughout Asia and became the source of popular literacy movements while Confucianist literacy remained the literacy of a powerful bureaucratic elite. According to O'Harrow, Confucianist literacy was much like the essayist literacy of Europe. It emphasized the text as absolute and inviolable. No copies were allowed to be made that were not made exactly and elegantly. Calligraphy was emphasized so that even the aesthetic appearance of the text would be reproduced. This kept literacy effectively restricted to an elite group of court-trained scholars who were the instruments of the distribution of court power. Literacy was transmitted through obedience, training, and normative standards.

Buddhist literacy, on the other hand, was characterized by a looseness in regard to the text. Oral interpretation and elaboration were necessary for understanding. Not only copying for dissemination but also translation were fostered. It was in this tolerance of deviation from the original text that the way was opened for popular literacy movements. Anyone could write who chose to, and ultimately scripts developed which were only distantly related to their sources.

It is probably dangerous to seek too many parallels in the West or to develop these differences further here. What seems significant to us is that both of these traditions were developed throughout Asia, and as far as we know were never strictly in competition. There was probably something more like a functional specialization of these types of literacy than the enshrinement of one type as the only access to knowledge. We suggest that in our search for understanding of the dominance of essayist literacy in European society it will ultimately be important to look further into traditions outside Europe.

The Role of Scripts

We have suggested, following O'Harrow, that the development of popular literacy and scripts in Asia evolved out of the Buddhist literacy tradition and its open attitude toward change and innovation. Chao (1968) has argued that the use of Chinese writing, while it may greatly increase learning time, gives a facility in reading that more than compensates for the effort spent in learning. Havelock (1963) has attributed the development of Greek thought in the early period to the development of alphabetic writing, and although Goody and Watt (1963) continued this argument, Goody (1968, 1977) more recently has played down the importance of the actual script.

It seems important to keep the arena open for investigation because some cases of native American literacy have involved non-alphabetic scripts. The syllabic script developed by the Wesleyan missionary Evans has been used widely in Canada by the Crees, for whom it was invented, but also by Chipewyans and Inuit. In the Kutchin area McDonald (1911) developed an alphabetic system but insisted that his experience had led him to feel that only a syllabary was effective in teaching literacy. The longstanding strength of Kutchin literacy in the system developed by McDonald attests to factors that we must seek to understand.

Vai Literacy

In an attempt to begin to sort out the range of factors relating literacy, schooling, and cognition, Scribner and Cole (1978a,b, Scribner 1979) have been involved in a study of literacy in Africa. They have described a situation in which three types of literacy exist together. The Vai script is phonetic and has been used for over a century for personal and village public needs. It is learned in informal contexts without schooling. Arabic literacy is associated with the learning of the Qur'an and is learned through a long process of schooling which consists to an important extent on the memorization of the Qur'an. English literacy is associated with schooling outside the village. Students go away to school and learn English as part of a full twelve-year curriculum of European education.

Scribner and Cole have described important functional differences in these literacies. They are used differently and learned differently. They have further argued that there are important cognitive consequences of these literacies. They have shown the best experimental evidence to date that there are language and cognitive skills that are directly related to reading and writing. In this work our interest is not in the cognitive consequences of literacy so much as in the social consequences. We are concerned with seeing how a particular form of literacy is related to personal and social identity. It is clear from Scribner and Cole's work that there is some social distribution of the three literacies of the Vai, and it is our goal to suggest that the factors that associate English schooling with essayist literacy are factors relating to discourse.

ESSAYIST LITERACY AS DISCOURSE PATTERNS

Both from the history of literacy in the western world (Goody 1977) and from Scribner and Cole's work in Africa it is clear that as a new phenomenon, literacy is radically dissociated from language as text. The first uses of writing have historically been the preparation of various kinds of lists. Language as label has been the entrance of writing into relation with speech. After a period of time the earliest uses of writing to represent longer stretches of speech have been in such things as recipes or letters. For the Vai it is the newest form of literacy, the Vai script, that is used in this function. We would suggest that at the beginning writing is highly decontextualized in its separation from speech. The objects listed occur in their juxtaposition only on the list, not in nature. The kings listed in succession do not and could not ever stand in a representative line. As writing is used for letters, speaking and writing become more closely aligned. It is speaking that dictates the form of the written text. The final development that follows, at least in Europe, has been the transformation of discourse into the decontextualization of writing.

DECONTEXTUALIZATION OF DISCOURSE

We have discussed some of the changes in writing in the shift to essayist literacy. The ideal text is closed to alternative interpretation. It is non-indexical. Nothing outside the text is needed for interpretation. These factors have important implications for the discourse structure. The important relationships to be signaled are those between sentence and sentence, not those between speakers nor those between sentence and speaker. As reader this requires a constant monitoring of grammatical and lexical information. The listener can get a good bit of meaning from the situational context in spoken discourse. In reading essayist prose the contextual clues to interpretation are in the text itself.

New and given information in essayist prose are signaled syntactically and lexically, not prosodically as in English speech. This requires a higher attention to syntax and especially to sequential relations among sentences. At the same time there is a higher percentage of new information in essayist prose. As Cook-Gumperz and Gumperz (1978) point out, it takes much longer to say something than to read an equivalent written statement. This difference in redundancy requires a much higher degree of attention to essayist prose than to speech.

With the heightened emphasis on truth value rather than social or rhetorical conditions, comes necessity to be explicit about logical implications. The logical relations of sentences in essayist prose must be explicitly marked, which again requires a heightened attention as well as the monitoring of longer sequences of text.

A significant aspect of the essayist prose style is the fictionalization of both the audience (Ong 1977) and the author (Foucault 1977b). We have said that within the essayist text it is the text itself that provides the contexts for the interpretation of the text. Rather than saying it is decontextualized, we might say it is reflexively contextualized. This same relationship holds true between texts. Ong (1977) has argued that writing only speaks to other writing. The process of reflexive contextualization continues outside the text into the universe of writing. The "reader" of an essayist text is not an ordinary human being. It is an idealization, a rational mind formed by the rational body of knowledge of which the essay is a part. The reader is not allowed lapses of attention or idiosyncrasies. By the

48

same token, the author is a fiction. The author as a person, by a process of writing and editing, seeks to achieve a state of self-effacement. The author seeks to write as a clear communication from rational mind to rational mind. It is assumed in this fictionalization of author and audience that any obstruction in the pure view of truth is the result of faults in the text, of its being less than a perfect representation of knowledge. In this process of refinement each text speaks to each previously created text and the author and reader stand to the discourses of text as human facilitators.

THE MODERN CONSCIOUSNESS AND ESSAYIST LITERACY

Among the defining properties of the modern consciousness given by Berger, Berger and Kellner (1973), *rationality, componentiality,* and *plurality* are strikingly like the attributes of essayist literacy. The ideal of essayist literacy that all meaning resides in the text is of course impossible to achieve. As an ideal, however, it expresses a view of the world as rational and of an identity between rational knowledge and linguistic expression (Foucault 1973). The ultimate knowability of the real world is matched by the assumption of its complete expressibility in text. One has only to observe clearly and think clearly, and clear expression will follow automatically.

Componentiality of all units of reality is assumed by the modern consciousness. One's own role in this reality is equally componentialized. All aspects of reality are assumed to be clearly bounded, isolable, and imply structural interchangeability. Berger, Berger and Kellner point out the interchangeability of individual workers in the bureaucratic and technological modern institutions as further examples of componentiality extending to personal roles.

Essayist literacy has been characterized as decontextualized in relation to situations. The text is a bounded, isolable entity. Within the text the grammar is assumed to work by equally componential structural principles. The logic of syntactic cohesion dominates essayist text. Vagueness and indexicality are ruled out. One can see the development of structural studies of grammar as a strong representation of the componentiality of the modern consciousness.

It is interesting in this context to compare Goody's (1977) argument that the historical foundation of literacy and ultimately of essayist literacy is the list or table. The visual display of nouns in the array of the table is according to Goody a significant precursor of classification. Classification and the componentiality of the modern consciousness may of course be seen as highly compatible if not identical.

The plurality of the modern consciousness is, according to Berger, Berger and Kellner, unique only in the extreme to which it is carried. They suggest that some conceptualization of multiple worlds is characteristic of all humans. To the modern consciousness, however, plurality is an essential theme. There is in fact no *world*, but only *worlds*. This pluralism is reinforced in the plurality of social roles that the individual enacts in his ordinary affairs. In this plurality, again, we see a parallel with the fictionalization of author and audience in essayist literacy. While all communication may require some plurality of communicative roles (Goffman 1974, 1979), it is clear that the high degree of self-effacement required of the author in essayist literacy as well as the fictionalization of the audience in the concept of the reading public carries this pluralization and fictionalization of communicative roles to an extreme.

In short, we are suggesting that there is a high degree of compatibility between the concepts of the modern consciousness as a reality set and essayist literacy as a set of discourse patterns and even as a cognitive style. We suggest that they are in fact alternate expressions of the same phenomenon from perhaps somewhat different perspectives.

We suggested in our discussion of the modern consciousness and the bush consciousness at Fort Chipewyan (Scollon & Scollon 1979) that while on the whole these reality sets characterized the world-view of individuals, there was a tendency for individuals to seek a personal negotiation between the two reality sets. In this work we will be treating the two reality sets as conceptually distinct and seek to show how at least in their broad outlines the reality sets are internally consistent and to a considerable degree mutually contradictory.

In spite of the mutually contradictory nature of the modern consciousness and the bush consciousness, many contexts in modern northern life appear to require a shift from one orientation to the other. We know of individuals who are in fact quite successful in negotiating this exchange of reality sets to at least the extent that they can and do become functional in either context. On the whole, though, it appears to be rare that any individual feels completely at home in both reality sets and we know of none who feel very comfortable in situations requiring something like simultaneous management of both points of view.

As we will seek to show in chapter four for the modern consciousness and in chapter six for the bush consciousness, each reality set is the result of significant learning and experience with others who share that orientation. Because of the depth of this learning and the normally early age at which it takes place, change comes equally slowly and appears to require similar learning contexts of concerned, nurturing members to guide one's development.

We have suggested that the modern consciousness shares significant characteristics with what we have called essayist literacy. It is beyond the scope of this study to go any further into the history of ideas to seek origins. Berger, Berger and Kellner argue that the modern consciousness is a product of modern bureaucratic and technological institutions. Goody (1977) suggests that those institutions themselves are products of the literate orientation begun many centuries earlier. Foucault (1973, 1977a) does not seek causes in earlier historical periods but sees a set of logical implications among modern social and technological institutions such as the factory, the school, the prison, the zoological garden, the military, and structures of modern thought as represented in historical-comparative linguistics, grammatical analysis, psychotherapy, ethnography, biology, and medicine. The modern development of literature and what we are calling essayist literacy Foucault sees as part of this "episteme" or logically interrelated period in the history of ideas. While the roots are certainly ancient the present configuration is a modern phenomenon.

ESSAYIST LITERACY AS
ENGLISH DISCOURSE PATTERNS

We described in the preceding chapter several properties of discourse in Athabaskan–English interethnic communication. Now we would like to suggest that the modern consciousness best represents the reality set of the English speaker in such dyads while the bush consciousness represents the reality set of the Athabaskan. Again, we want to emphasize that we are not suggesting that all

English speakers speak always and only from the point of view of the modern consciousness nor that all Athabaskans speak always and only from the point of view of the bush consciousness. As distinct cases on which to build the discussion it is necessary for the moment to assume such extreme isomorphism. In the real world of communication cases are not often so distinct.

The ideal essayist text is an explicit, decontextualized presentation of a view of the world that fictionalizes both author and audience. There is a high level of new information and the internal structure is cohesive and clearly bounded. As we have shown in the preceding chapter, to the Athabaskan, the English speaker presents as well a fictionalized self and speaks in long, bounded, topic-controlled monologues. These monologues are the result of the English preference for speaking first, the fact that the first speaker controls the topic, and the shorter pause taken at the end of each turn by the English speaker. The Athabaskan finds it difficult in these interactions to introduce a topic and if he succeeds it continues to be difficult to maintain the floor. The result of these mechanical factors coupled with different preferences for the use of talk in encounters with strangers is the English-speaker monologue.

As we compare the features of English discourse in Athabaskan –English interethnic communication with the essayist prose style we see a high degree of similarity. To the Athabaskan the English speaker does "talk like a book."

We should note that the bookishness of the English monologue is a result of the specifically interethnic nature of the communication. In strictly English–English conversation the factors that lead to monologic presentations are controlled by a more even exchange of turns and a general agreement on the nature and goals of conversation. In this case, however, interethnic communication produces speech in which language dominates the situation, language creates its own contexts of interpretation, and language speaks to the future and other situations. These features all shared in common with the essayist prose style give to English discourse a figure much like that of writing.

As we have suggested in the preceding chapter, the Athabaskan response to these features is ethnic stereotyping of the English speaker as smug, boastful, and too talkative. Now we would like to extend this to suggest that for the Athabaskan, essayist text appears much the same. We suggest that the Athabaskan cannot engage in reading or writing essayist prose without developing some of the same stereotypes of arrogance and irrelevance. As a reader this may not be so critical but let us consider the problem of writing.

WRITING AS A CRISIS IN ETHNIC IDENTITY

For an Athabaskan to produce an essay would require him or her to produce a major display. This display would be appropriate only if the person was in a position of dominance in relation to the audience. But as we have said, the audience, and the author, are fictionalized in essayist prose. The text itself becomes decontextualized. This means that the clear relationship of dominance is obscured. Where the relationship of the communicants is unknown we have said the Athabaskan prefers silence. The paradox of prose for the Athabaskan then is that to the extent that it is a communication between known author and audience it is contextualized and therefore not good essayist prose. To the extent that it becomes decontextualized it becomes more uncharacteristic of Athabaskans to seek to communicate.

The Athabaskan set of discourse patterns are to a large extent mutually exclusive of the discourse patterns of essayist prose. In order to write, the Athabaskan must adopt discourse patterns that are identified with a particular ethnic group, identified in Alaska and Canada as English speakers.

This dilemma becomes critical where writing is in native languages for distinctly native purposes. While we would note that Athabaskan speakers speaking from a position of authority easily create remarkably coherent "texts" on Athabaskan subjects, we would argue that an Athabaskan cannot, as an Athabaskan, write easily about Athabaskan things. It is only to the extent that he or she is modernized, has come to identify as an English speaker, that he or she can operate within the essayist ideal of literacy. Where the interethnic communication patterns produce social conflict between speakers these same patterns produce internal conflict for an Athabaskan writer. We suggest it is this internal conflict that explains much of the problem of native literacy programs as well as problems with English literacy in the public school systems of Alaska and Canada.

Kutchin Literacy

There is an obvious difficulty with the statements we have just made. For many years Kutchin Athabaskans have enjoyed an important native literacy. We would now like to consider this apparent exception. For example, Albert Tritt at Arctic Village, Alaska, kept an extensive and detailed journal (Tritt nd) for many years. Early in this century, he saw literacy in Kutchin and the Episcopal faith as the only way his people would survive the crushing pressures of modernization. His work was part of a more general Anglican/Episcopal religious movement spurred by Archdeacon Robert McDonald from the Canadian Kutchin area. People today remember sitting around campfires while the old people recited the syllabary prepared by McDonald in his alphabetic writing of Kutchin.

While we do not yet have an adequate history of this early Kutchin literacy we do know enough to suggest why it should have been as successful as it was. If we recall the three types of literacy described by Scribner and Cole (1978a) we can see that what we have called essayist literacy corresponds to English literacy for the Vai. Kutchin literacy, on the other hand, is much like Qur'anic literacy.

For the Kutchin, literacy was reading the Bible. It was on the whole unilateral. That is, one read but did not write liturgical materials. The goal was the faithful adoption of the truth of the word. To the extent writing was used it was used to practice for copying out of the Bible, and for keeping a record of religious activities. The work of Albert Tritt may be explained by his own conviction that he was an important leader of his people. He could risk the assumption of the authorship role on behalf of his people.

As a secondary development writing became used by the Kutchin for many of the pragmatic uses that Vai literacy performs. Students learned to read by listening to a teacher read from the Bible, hymn book, or prayer book. On the side, however, they began to practice by writing notes and letters to each other. The students invented a pragmatic Vai-type literacy spontaneously out of the Qur'anic Kutchin religious literacy, and this pragmatic literacy is still functioning to some extent.

We can see now that both Qur'anic and Vai-type literacies

avoid the problems of ethnic identity that befall essayist literacy. In the first case, the word as handed down from a divine source fits into the Athabaskan pattern of dominance being associated with display. It is appropriate for God to deliver messages to man, not vice versa. At the same time the non-critical attitude is appropriate in relation to God's Word and fits the Athabaskan pattern of the subordinate or learner as spectator.

Vai-type pragmatic literacy on the other hand occurs between people well known to each other. It is highly contextualized and depends absolutely on each participant reading between the lines. Another factor that might be mentioned is that there is no normative standard. Because it is contextualized, spelling may be idiosyncratic and still be interpreted correctly. Vai-type literacy is well suited to the underground, unofficial or informal mode of learning and transmission. Students invented this form of letter writing as a non-serious use of the serious Qur'anic style literacy and could be much freer in their spelling and grammar.

In summary then, we can see that Kutchin literacy has been successful to the extent it has because it has not been essayist literacy. Vai-type literacy and Qur'anic type literacy appear to be compatible with Athabaskan discourse patterns. Learning literacy in these patterns does not threaten to produce changes in ethnic identity the way essayist literacy does. Essayist literacy in any language may in fact be a powerful instrument of cultural and ethnic change.

THE NEED FOR FURTHER STUDY

We have advanced in this chapter a number of suggestions relating interethnic communication and three types of literacy. We now would like to emphasize that we have used the word "suggest" intentionally. While programs for the development of literacy have been rapidly proliferating in Alaska and Canada, the study of literacy has not been well established. The suggestions that we have advanced are based on the research that has been done as well as on our own interpretation of that research and the history as it is now known of various literacies. Rather than "findings" we would like to regard our suggestions here as hypotheses that could be studied in ongoing research.

It is clear that we need a much fuller understanding of Kutchin literacy both past and present. We need to carefully research both interethnic communication and literacy training to test for the accuracy of the parallels we have drawn here.

Finally, we should emphasize that here we have spoken only of Athabaskan–English interethnic communication and literacy. There is a critical need to understand interethnic communication among other groups in Alaska and Canada and a further need to seek to relate these patterns to literacy. If literacy relates as closely to discourse patterns as we believe it does, then other native groups which have quite obviously different discourse patterns can be expected to relate in different ways to literacy.

Four

The Literate Two-Year-Old: The Fictionalization of Self

We have suggested that the modern consciousness, the discourse patterns of essayist literacy, and the spoken discourse of English speakers in interethnic communication with Athabaskans are expressions of the same fundamental phenomenon. We have also argued that these patterns are internally consistent and learned through a process of socialization and experience with others who share these orientations. Now we will describe a case study of how a child learned and was taught the fictionalization of self required for the modern consciousness and essayist literacy.

MAKING THE ORDINARY REMARKABLE

For many of us the contexts in which we raise our children are quite unremarkable. They seem to be ordinary children growing up in the ordinary way. We see language learning as a natural part of this growing up and do not think further about it. It is the task of research in children's language to make this ordinary process problematical so that we can see how it is constituted. In our previous research on children's language we had learned two things. The first was that there was much more going on in the early stages of language learning than we had thought (Scollon 1976a). The unfolding of this natural development was carefully constructed in

57

interactions between the caregiver and the child. Things did not simply happen.

The second thing we had learned had been much harder to deal with in terms of research. At Arctic Village, Alaska, we had learned that children were not learning to speak by means of the same process as the very ordinary children who had been described by us and by other researchers in the literature. That is, there was either something wrong with the children, which we rejected as an expression of the unacceptable cultural deficit hypothesis, or there was something wrong with our concept of "ordinary."

For some time we thought that the most effective way to study this problem would be to do studies of language learning in other cultural settings. We began a year of field research at Fort Chipewyan, Alberta[1] (Scollon & Scollon 1979) in 1976. Among our goals was the study of language learning at Forth Chipewyan. We planned to directly address the problem of cultural differences in language socialization. In our work we were accompanied by our daughter Rachel, for whom pseudonymity would be pointless in this case.[2] She was two years and three months old when our work began and had passed three when it was finished.

As our work progressed we began to see that our ordinary means of interacting with our own child had become very remarkable, not in having changed but by contrast to patterns and expectations in the community of Fort Chipewyan. It was we ourselves who had been placed into research focus by our relocation. In this paper then we will be treating at some length the linguistic socialization of our own child. Although this implies a commitment on our part to a set of communicative patterns for our own children, we do not wish to suggest in any way that we feel this pattern is the only set of patterns we wish to have available to our children. Our children have also had a deep involvement with Asian communicative patterns and through their experience at Fort

[1] This research was supported during July and August 1976 by the Summer Stipend Program of the National Endowment for the Humanities, and from September 1976 to August 1977 by the Urgent Ethnology Programme of the National Museum of Man, National Museums of Canada, Ottawa. The support of these agencies is gratefully acknowledged.

[2] Rachel was born April 4, 1974. This is the first report of our research on her communicative development which began at birth. Our primary focus in this research was on patterns of communicative interaction during the first year. Documentation has been with photographs, audio tapes and written observational notebooks.

Chipewyan and in Alaska with native American communicative patterns. Our children are literate in the sense described herein. We are not seeking to create an invidious comparison with the children of Fort Chipewyan in this work by pointing to contrasts. We are very concerned, however, with finding the means of understanding cultural and communicative differences and relating these to issues of ethnic identity.

The Cross-examination

One evening several boys about ten years of age brought a box into our house with two crippled mice in it. They had caught them and were having fun playing with them while they died. When Rachel looked into the box R. Scollon asked her how many mice there were. She said there were two mice. One of the boys then asked R. Scollon what school Rachel was going to.

Our point here is that we thought there was nothing remarkable about asking and expecting a correct answer to our question. The boys, on the other hand, took either Rachel's ability to answer or her willingness to respond to cross-examination as evidence for schooling even though they knew how old she was, knew that there was no school in Fort Chipewyan for two year old children, and in fact probably knew all the children in the one preschool and the one elementary school. We will argue in this paper that what was important in this case was the cross-examination, the interactive pattern that these boys associated with schooling, so strongly in fact that they could overlook obvious things such as Rachel's size in presenting this explanation.

A Puzzle

It is not difficult to elaborate instances in which Rachel's orientation to "school" tasks was noticeably different from that of children at Fort Chipewyan. At two, if given the time, she assembled children's jigsaw puzzles. She did this on the basis of shape as much as color or picture, and said as much. Frequently, visiting children tried to assemble Rachel's puzzle. Even though they started enthusiastically and could have gone on as long as they wanted, few of them ever produced a completed puzzle.

The comment of one boy of eight years of age is illustrative. One of the pieces had a uniform color. As he threw it aside he said, "It got no picture." It might be pointed out that there was only one puzzle and the boy knew this. Although we could make the mistake of arguing that he should have known that that piece must have belonged in the puzzle somewhere, we would rather suggest that his orientation to the task was radically different from Rachel's. We believe that this is the difference that these children themselves observe as an effect of schooling.

The Peer Teaching of Reading

A third example ties this association of Rachel's abilities to reading. A ten year old girl sat down with her younger sister, who was three and a half, and said she was going to teach her to read. The interaction back and forth echoed almost liturgically:

(Older sister)	OS:	because
(Younger sister)	YS:	because
	OS:	a
	YS:	a
	OS:	giraffe
	YS:	giraffe
	OS:	might
	YS:	might
	OS:	look
	YS:	look
	OS:	sort of
	YS:	sort of
	OS:	silly
	YS:	silly

Just a short time later the older sister sat down with Rachel saying she was now going to teach her as she had her own sister. She began in the same way.

	OS:	because
	RS:	because a goat might eat it for supper.
	OS:	The whole *thing!*

Rachel of course knew the book. It was hers and had been read for her a number of times. The ten year old though was both amazed and dismayed at Rachel's performance. After her outburst of surprise she worked at getting Rachel to give the echoed response her younger sister had given. After a few tries Rachel acquiesced and then wandered off to do something else.

We see in this example that Rachel's orientation is both very different and inappropriate by Fort Chipewyan standards. At two years of age she was an anomaly in the eyes of other children.

"SCHOOL" AS A GLOSS FOR LITERACY

As we have said in chapter three, Olson (1977b) has advanced the argument that literacy has been both the medium and the goal of schooling in western society and that this orientation has specific consequences for cognition and knowledge. We have looked at the varieties of literacy suggested by Scribner and Cole (1978a) and at their suggestion that each may have its own consequences in the structure of knowledge. We have suggested that a specific form of literacy, what we have called essayist literacy, may be characterized as having the properties that Olson and others (Cook– Gumperz & Gumperz 1978; Goody 1977) have attributed to literacy in general. The essential properties we suggest are decontextualization through fictionalization of authorship (Foucault 1977b) and readership (Ong 1977), and decontextualization through the internal cohesion of the information structure (Cook–Gumperz & Gumperz 1978).

Here we will argue that the reactions to Rachel's "schooling" were in fact reactions to her incipient literacy. We will argue that Rachel was in most ways literate before she learned to read, that for her learning to read was little more than learning spelling conventions because of the systematic preparation in the literate orientation that we had given her. As a central aspect of this orientation we will further suggest the importance of the fictionalization of the self required for literacy. Finally we will describe some of the ways in which this literacy is trained in interactions with caregivers.

LOCATING LITERACY

Literacy is no simple matter. As a phenomenon it is located in a complex of behaviors, attitudes, situations, values, institutions, and personal roles. Although we do not wish to suggest that there is any unique location of literacy in any society to which all members would agree, it is clear that there is a good bit of typification to which a member has access. This typification of literacy becomes clearer as we observe both the socialization process and as we contrast variation of socialization. In this case it is striking how differently Rachel and people at Fort Chipewyan have typified or located literacy. This typification in fact appears to be the entry point for socialization to literacy.

Reading is a Matter of Hands

Rachel was trying to get her mother to read to her. Her mother told her to read it herself. Rachel asked "How I can read?" Her mother said, "With your eyes." She answered, "I can't hold books with my eyes." In later discussion she said her baby brother could not read because his hands were too small but would be able to when his hands grew. The dog, though, would never be able to read because he had no hands.

This example indicates some of the things that Rachel knew about literacy by two years of age. It amounted at least to reading. It was expected of humans and was about as natural as growing hands big enough to hold a book. For her, literacy was a natural part of the home, and one of the good things at that. She asked much more often to be read stories than to be given special foods.

Beyond this understanding of literacy Rachel knew it to involve writing. As we shall see in two examples that follow, she "wrote" her own stories to read and tape record. She had learned a definite oral reading prosody that was markedly different from her conversational prosody. Generally she expected letters to make sense if arranged linearly. Once she lined up seven wooden blocks with letters and said they spelled "SCOLLON." They did not, but the total and orientation was correct.

Rachel's typification of literacy by two years of age was essentially the same as ours. It was appropriate to all people. Children participated through play and through special child registers such as reading aloud. She had her own books, letter blocks, knew the "ABC" song, and fully expected to go to school when she was older. Literacy for her included the symmetrical balance between reading and writing. Readers were writers, and writers were readers in her view. It was appropriate for a child in a subordinate position to display abilities in literacy to adults and older children. It was also appropriate to listen to older people read. Literacy was something both assumed as a value and asserted as a right. For Rachel literacy was a central attribute and activity of human life.

Goffman's *Asylums* as a Song Book

Literacy was typified very differently at Fort Chipewyan. A seven year old boy after he knew us quite well took a copy of Goffman's *Asylums* off the shelf and asked, "You guys sing from this?" When we said that we did not he asked incredulously if we read it. Books at Fort Chipewyan are typically song books or prayer books used in church. The relationship to books is unidirectional. People are readers or singers but not writers. Literacy is strongly associated with religious contexts which at Fort Chipewyan are generally Roman Catholic.

Partly as a corollary of the location of literacy in the church, there is a strong feeling that only older people can or should read. The mother of the ten year old girl above who read to her younger sister and Rachel, told another daughter of hers when she picked up one of our books, "You can't read anyway. It's too high words for you." The child's interest was treated as being out of character.

To some extent literacy of this unidirectional sort is also associated with the school; but until recently the school was very closely associated with the mission at Fort Chipewyan and may not yet be regarded as a separate institution.

In the terms that could be developed from Scribner and Cole's (1978a) work, people at Fort Chipewyan typify literacy as Qur'anic rather than what we would call essayist literacy. As we have suggested in chapter two, there is an important relationship between dominance and display that affects the differences between Rachel's and the other children's typification of literacy. It is for us the dominant member of an asymmetrical pair who is spectator and the subordinate member who is exhibitor (Mead 1977, Bateson 1972). Thus it is appropriate for Rachel to develop elaborate displays of her knowledge of literacy. It is further appropriate for her as subordinate to the author of a text to read it aloud.

The relationship is reversed for Fort Chipewyan children. As we have suggested, at Fort Chipewyan it is the dominant member who displays and the subordinate who is spectator. In this configuration it is arrogant for a subordinate member to make any display. A child in relation to an adult should be quiet and reserved. As reader in relation to a text a child should only closely imitate or repeat in liturgical fashion but not presume to a full display of the text as a performance. In the same way the adult as reader in relation to the religious text cannot presume to subordinate God to his own position by elaborate displays of reading and much less assume an equivalent position by becoming an author, by writing.

The difference then between Rachel's typification of literacy and the typification held in general at Fort Chipewyan makes a striking contrast. This difference showed itself when after writing several stories Rachel tried to show them to two eight year old friends. She said, "I wrote down some stories." After a moment she went on, "It's about Goldilocks and the Three Bears and all kinds of other stories." The other children heard but chose to ignore Rachel's display. As in the case of the girl who intended to teach her to read, Rachel's behavior was inappropriate. They sought to correct her as they had been corrected by their elders, with silence.

As a way into literacy Rachel by two years of age had achieved a typification of a set of activities and behaviors, a distribution among social roles, and a set of values and attitudes that corresponded closely to ours. The other children at Fort Chipewyan had also achieved a typification, but it was a very different one. Literacy was inappropriate for children. For adults it was unidirectional, one read but did not write. Literacy was socially located not in the home but in the church and subsidiarily in the school. It was within this context of a different typification of literacy that we began to look more closely at how Rachel became literate.

LITERACY AS AUTOBIOGRAPHY

"We are all authors of a continual autobiography." (Hall 1973)

Goffman (1974) has emphasized the importance of the replayed nature of the presentation of self in ordinary conversation. As we talk we characterize ourselves for the others and ourselves to consider. We would further argue, following Hall's statement that there is something literate about this continual self-characterization, that it amounts to authorship. We will further argue following Foucault (1977b), Ong (1977), and Chatman (1978) that this continual authorship amounts to the fictionalization of the self as author, audience, and character that is so central to the literate orientation.

To do this we would like to consider two stories that Rachel wrote and read just a few days before her third birthday. It is significant, we feel, that she would not tell stories without writing them first. That is, for her, storytelling was reading. By the same token she insisted on reading out what she had written. She assumed an audience and succeeded in getting an audience for her writing. We suggested tape recording the readings, and from her initial willingness and subsequent insistence we see that this additional step of distance was well within the conceptualization she had of her activity.

All told there were eight stories and one recipe in the event from which the stories that follow were taken. The first was not recorded. The two following stories are the second and third in the sequence of eight.

RACHEL'S WRITTEN VERSION, STORY ONE

The stories were written on scraps of paper that were left over from some earlier drawing and cutting. In this case Rachel wrote the story out silently starting at the top left hand corner, writing left to right, top to bottom. The small marks just above the bottom right flourish were written last.

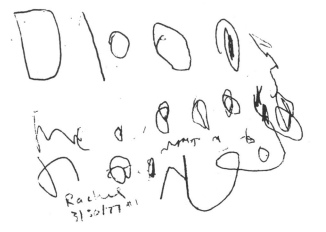

FIGURE 1. STORY ONE

Transcription of Story One

The following transcription gives the full frame surrounding this story as well as Rachel's reading. The following conventions have been used in this transcription:

a. A new line indicates a pause.
b. A double space with a dot (·) indicates a breath and a pause.
c. A comma (,) indicates a breath taken without a pause.
d. A right parenthesis) followed by a word indicates that the word was said with an ingressive airstream.
e. A hyphen indicates an interrupted word.
f. Double slashes (//) indicate a final intonation that is a high rising then falling contour (⌢⌍).
g. Triple slashes (///) indicate a final intonation that is a low long falling contour (————).
h. A question mark followed by double slashes (?//) indicates a final questioning intonation that is a low rising contour (⌣⌍).
i. Parentheses () indicate comments by her father.

Story One

> Rachel 3/30/77
> (OK now read me your story)
> Then you'll put it on?//
> (Uh huh)
> OK.
> There was a b–
> girl
> she
> went out to get snow //
> ·
> she
> she made a hole //
> ·
> she
> ·
> went back

she cried //

.

she went back in tell m-

.

)her
her Mom to get
tel(1)—old her Mom, to
give her apple //
so she gived her apple ///

.

she got

.

she went out again
got sn-
some more snow? //
(hey.)
Now put it on.
(OK.)

READING PROSODY

One of the major differences in English between speaking and writing is in the signaling of the information structure (Gumperz 1977b, Gumperz & Roberts 1978). In speaking, the information structure is signaled prosodically through tone grouping, nucleus placement, stress and pitch change. In writing none of these mechanisms is available and the information structure must be indicated grammatically, lexically, and through such conventions as paragraphing and especially in children's stories the spacing and distribution on the printed page.

Reading intonation represents intermediate prosody. The intonation structure is explicit in the text itself because the text is written. Reading intonation, then, must introduce prosodic features of ordinary speech for the sake of sounding "natural" but at the same time must not signal ordinary conversational processes such as turn taking.

From Rachel's reading of this text we can see both her concern to maintain the sound of a complex, explicit, written information structure and to preclude any possibility of conversational intonation. The contours indicated with double slash (//) indicate simultaneously the close of information units and the intention to continue reading. As falling contours they correspond to conversational information closures but as high pitches they signal a holding, an intention to go on. By the same token the finality of the /// close is negated by the length and slowness of the pitch fall. It is controlled, not allowed to drop off as in conversation.

Before we look at further details it is important to recall that Rachel's "reading" is not really a reading. She is not trying to represent a structure that exists prior to the telling. Instead she is trying to sound like that is what she is doing. She is trying to sound like she is reading. It is a global performance of a style of language use. The prosody which is derived from adult oral reading is in this case the symbol of that reading. It has no actual content.

It is all the more remarkable that she does not use any of the usual conversational hesitation markers. There are no *um*'s and very few recyclings of phrases while she plans what to say next. Where she does hesitate or recycle she prosodically holds onto the information structure. As an example we can look at the very opening line. She begins to say "boy" and then shifts to "girl." Even though there is a pause and a breath, Rachel does not recycle to "there was a girl." This given information "there was a" is held prosodically while the new information is corrected and the phrase then continues to its end at "snow//."

This whole phrase is prosodically what it would have been if she had said, "There was a girl who went out to get snow." In this case "she" is not a recycling nor does it begin a new sentence. "She" is functionally equivalent to the relative pronoun "who" and is treated prosodically as such.

A further case is in the sentence where she begins to say "tell Mommy" and then corrects to "tell her Mom" which is further corrected to "told her Mom." Her choice was something like "she went back in to tell her Mom to give her an apple" against "she went back in and told her Mom to give her an apple." The resolution is to the grammatically simpler conjunction with "and." In this case she had to take two breaths to get the whole unit said. In the first case she breathes in on ")her," in the second she breathes without pausing. When she shifts "tell" to "told" she does not even recycle the whole word but rather turns the *l*, which is phonetically [ε^{u}] into [$\varepsilon^{u}o^{u}$] to get "told." Throughout, the prosody is that of the whole unit. One feels that she is under considerable pressure to create clearly bounded information units without hesitation, interruption or recycling. These would be the units so characteristic of written text which is known to Rachel in the form of orally read text.

A good indication of this pressure Rachel felt to create a pro-sodically smooth performance is that when she read these texts she kicked her legs, squirmed on her chair, bobbed her head back and forth rhythmically, and generally showed all the signs of great con-centration and energy. The next day when she "read" "Goldilocks and the Three Bears" on a tape recording for her grandparents she refused to sit. She could only bring off the performance standing with room to move around. This is in marked contrast to her prefer-ence for sitting quietly for conversation.

In the instance where Rachel read "Goldilocks and the Three Bears" she forgets one line. On the tape we hear ("TAP TAP TAP) house//." That is, she fills in the memory gap with a sequence of taps and finished out the phrase with the one word she remembered complete with final, closing intonation. Only in the last sentence does Rachel shift to the conversational "?//" intonation. Here she gives up the floor and requests interaction with her father. Both in holding the floor prosodically and then conversationally giving it up she shows her control of the reading intonation.

We can see from the example, then, that Rachel had a good understanding of the nature of the relationship between oral reading prosody and the explicit intonation structure of written text. She felt for her performance to count as reading it had to move inexorably forward without hesitation, recyclings, or ungrammati-calities. Since a two year old could not meet all of the requirements it is important that she chose to keep the prosodic markings of the information structure inviolate and let other components such as the grammaticality of her performance falter.

The Fictionalization of Self

In this story about the girl who went out to get snow, cried to get an apple, and then returned to her task Rachel is author, char-acter, and audience. This event had happened to her on one of the preceding days. She was the girl who regularly collected snow for water and yet in her telling she takes the distance of the third person. It is "a girl," "she," "her Mom" and so on with one exception. Rachel begins to say "she went back in to tell Mommy." At "Mommy" she hesitates, corrects to "her Mom" and continues. She is not only assuming the third person in regard to herself, she is doing this carefully as part of her creation of the read text. As author she is Rachel. As character she is "a girl."

In another story there was the following passage:

Then I
showed them the pears
Then-
I uh-
Then first Rachel ate some

Again, Rachel slips into the first person in this self-characterization and then corrects to the third person. It might be suggested that the first person becomes rather overpowering when the author has to recount details of suffering or pleasure but it is to her credit as an author that she is able to regain the balance in her point of view and keep it consistent throughout the narrative.

We would argue then that Rachel had understood by this time the essential distance of authorship from the text. The character in regard to the author is a different person. It is a decontextualized person. It is a person who exists in relationship to the text and the events told in it. This person bears a third person relationship to the author and this consistent maintenance of the point of view is one of the hallmarks of written text.

We would also like to follow Foucault (1977b) and further argue that by virtue of reciprocity the author has become a third person in relationship to the character of the text and to the text itself. Autobiography is the real test. To the extent that the author fictionalizes himself as character he fictionalizes himself as author as well. It is this essential fictionalization of the self involved in authorship that Rachel is capturing in her stories. As with the prosodic marking of information structure it is probably best to consider her work at this level to be based on models and not yet to involve a deep fictionalization of the self. Nevertheless her care in correcting slips in point of view, especially when they center on some emotional involvement, shows a movement in the direction of the fictionalization of authorship and we believe ultimately of the self. Rachel at this stage is structurally interchangeable with Goldilocks. To the extent Goldilocks becomes part of her world she becomes part of Goldilocks' world.

By the same token, Rachel's interest in recording this story and the others speaks for her fictionalization of herself as audience as well. Ong (1977) has argued that the writer's audience is always a fiction. In this case Rachel as listener reinforces the fictionalization of Rachel as character and as author. This three-way distribution of literacy roles indicates that Rachel is well on her way to full literacy.

RACHEL'S WRITTEN VERSION, STORY TWO

In the second story we will look at we can see that Rachel had a good understanding of the relationship between the written symbols and the read text even though she herself was still years from being able to decode it. As she wrote the text that follows she spoke to herself. The beginning section of the transcription includes her pronouncing of the letters as she wrote. She does not say all of them nor get them all right by any means. It is clear, however, that she is her own critic. This is shown by several self-corrections and by an occasional "I think" as she wrote a letter out.

Throughout this section her intonation is a slow rising (⌒) pitch, the "listing" or "roll call" intonation. She closes off the writing very clearly with "Yep!."

Rachel's pronouncing of the letters may seem an obvious thing to do until we ask why she did not attempt to pronounce out an intermediate level of words or sentences as well. We think she understands that the relationship between letters and the ultimate text is complex, mediated by a grammar and therefore does not seek to represent an intermediate level in any overt way. She goes directly from the written symbol to the read text.

Transcription of Story Two

The conventions in this transcription are the same as in the first story with one addition. A single slash (/) is used to indicate a non-final high falling (⌁) intonation which is very much like the intonation indicated by double slash (//).

FIGURE 2.   STORY TWO

When I write that story you tape record it?
(Yep)
After?
(Uh huh)
OK.

.

'I'

.

'C'
'D'
xxx
no 'I'

.

and um

.

.

'D'

.

'O'

.

and

.

'H'

.

'I'
'O'

.

and

.

uh

.

'L'
and
I think 'R'

.

and um

.

'O'

.

um
'D' I think
um

.

'O'

.

'I'

.

'I'

.

'I'
I think

Yep!

.

Now

.

Read this kind of story =   (= = high but not question)

.

(OK)
Story
(That's your story, OK?)
yeah
(You gonna read it?)
yeah
(OK)

.

or–this is about Baby Tommy and me!
(Oh, OK)

.

and you
(OK)

.

Once upon a time
there was a girl named Rachel and

.

and there was a boy / named Tommy //

.

the went f-
for a walk and there was Da- /
.) ddy
he went for a walk too //

.

They-

.

-ey wrote a-
letter

.

down
to

.

.

Baby Tommy's

.

Grandma //

.

she
Baby Tommy had a n-

.

Baby Tommy had a

.

fish xxx //
she

.

and he had a Mom //

.

his Mom

.

told him
to read his story ///

.

and his Mom
m-
tell him No! ///

.

You
go to sleep

.

and then
Baby Tommy went to sleep

He yelled
he cried //

.

And his Mom and Dad came

.

and they sayed, "what's the matter?"

.

and he s-

.

My girlfriend gived
me a apple /

.

and that's
that's
all. ///
(That's the end?)
Yeah.
(OK)
It's just written down right there.

Framing

This story is framed more carefully than the first story. It begins first with what we have called a performance frame (Scollon & Scollon 1979). That is, before beginning the story, Rachel tells her father what it will be about. We see this as giving an indication to the audience of how the whole is to be taken. It sets the reading apart as a different kind of event or genre than the ongoing conversation. This performance frame is closed when she says at the end "It's just written down right there." She refers by "it" to the text and the reading. Her reference here is the same as in the opening of the performance frame where she says "This is about-." By means of the frame she closes off a unit of the ongoing activity as a reading performance. This is a further example of her location of literacy. She locates it as a genre of verbal performance.

Within the performance frame the story itself is framed as a text. It has an opening frame or an initial. This is the traditional children's story formula "Once upon a time." This formula is cut off with a pause. In addition the word "time" is said with slight rising contour (⁀)which sounds like both a continuation marker and a listing intonation. It sounds as if Rachel is intending to isolate this formula to call attention to it. At any rate, the opening is formally marked. The final is equally well framed with "that's all."

Rachel's use of these story frames shows that not only is she aware of the oral performance genre but also she is aware of the children's story genre. These are two different things and independent to some extent. She has taken the care to mark both.

Prosodic Grouping

We see Rachel's concern for the primacy of the prosodic group in this story as in the first. Early in the story there is the long group "There was a girl named Rachel and there was a boy / named Tommy //." In the next group she seeks to make a parallel structure and runs into trouble on "Daddy" by running out of breath. She finishes the word on an ingressive airstream and closes out the phrase. This complete subordination of basic breathing patterns is something that bespeaks the concern for control of the intonation structure.

Just following this example Rachel begins by saying "They." As she hesitates, presumably to think up the next line, she even takes two breaths before she continues with an extension of "they" on the same pitch and in the same voice quality as she had left off. She continues rather than saying "um" or recycling completely as "they wrote." This phrase is not actually finished for another four breaths but the tone group is kept completely intact.

Another thing might be point out here. When Rachel begins this tone group she does not have any apparent idea how it is going to end. One thing is certain, however, it must begin with "they." It must begin with an anaphoric reference to the three characters set up in the first two tone groups. Again, Rachel shows considerable understanding of the dictates of explicit textural structuring and is seeking to embody that understanding in her reading performance. It might be said that her concern for information structure overrides her concern for plot. It is after all an odd thing to go for a walk in the woods and write a letter while doing so. If something has to give in reconciling all the factors of the reading performance, she appears to have chosen not to let the information structure weaken.

Another example of Rachel's use of a continued morpheme rather than recycling to indicate continuity of information structure came out of a reading of "Goldilocks and the Three Bears." At one point she said,

> There she
>
> .
>
> saw
> the thr-
> three bears
>
> .
>
> she-
> uh,
>
> .
>
> s house
> she peeked into the house

In this case the model in the story she was recalling was "there she saw the house of the three bears. She peeked into the house" (Playmore Edition, n.d.). It appears that she started to say "the three bears' house" then perhaps intended to correct to "the house of the three bears." That solution if it was in fact what she thought of, would have required major recycling. She apparently did consider going back to "she" but gave that up. Her solution was to stick with the phrase as she had begun it and this picking up again of the lost prosodic thread is indicated by "s house." She continues the last segment of "bears" from two lines earlier and keeps the prosodic and information unit together.

One last example of the independence of the prosodic and information structure from Rachel's reading comes from a comparison of two readings of the "Goldilocks" story.

> Oh my! I'm *hungry*
>)she
> thought to herself ///
>
> ---

oh my! I'm *hungry* she thought

)to

herself ///

This tone group in both cases takes two breaths and three pauses to assemble. The breath comes at a different place, however, in each case. The word which was said on the ingressive stream in each case was a different one. These are the only two words that are fully without stress in this phrase and were well selected as dispensable for the sake of the prosody. Otherwise the two phrases read on different days are virtually identical.

As in the first story, Rachel shows an overriding concern with the prosodic marking of information groups. Breathing, pausing, grammaticality, and even exact reproduction of the original are all subordinated to the production of informationally coherent text. The prosody marks her productions as reading even where she is creating the text as she goes. Rachel was well on her way to literacy by her third birthday in the sense of being able to create informationally decontextualized text.

Fictionalization of Self

In the second story Rachel even more strongly marks the fictionalization of herself as character and author. She has just said it was about "me" and "you" in the performance frame when she shifts to "Rachel" and "Daddy." In this we can see the boundary between the performance frame and the story frame as being a boundary in fictionalization.

Of course in this case the story itself is more vaguely related to Rachel's actual life. It is true that she and her father had walked in the woods recently, but the details of letter writing and the baby's sleeping are more purely fictitious. It is not surprising that Rachel is able to demarcate the boundaries more easily, then. No emotional involvement threatens to overpower the distance she is able to take from herself.

At the same time this story indirectly incorporates very current events. Just after mentioning the letter to the baby's grandmother the baby himself who had been napping began to cry. The line "Baby Tommy had a n-" may indicate an integration of his waking up from his nap into this account. Also, her suggestion in the narrative account that the baby was made to go back to sleep shows some further attempt to incorporate ongoing activity into her story. All accounts are fictionalized, however, by the use of the third person. Rachel as author as well as character remains at a third person distance from the crying baby.

Literacy as Content

A final detail might be mentioned. Literacy as content appears twice in this narrative. In the first place the threesome walking in the woods wrote a letter to the baby's grandmother. Writing for Rachel is a wholly natural activity. It is something that might occur anywhere, anytime. It is also appropriate for writers to exercise their skill on behalf of others who cannot, presumably because their hands are too small, write for themselves. In this detail she expresses her general location of literacy, which we have already discussed.

In the second instance although it seems grammatically confused, she says that the baby wished to have a story read to him. Again, we see the value Rachel places on having stories read. It ranks with being given apples among the pleasures of life.

A CONTRASTING CASE

To set Rachel's developing literacy into perspective we will look at one example of a story by a ten year old Chipewyan girl at Fort Chipewyan. This story is one of many we might have used but was chosen here because it was suitably brief. The girl is the one referred to earlier as "Older sister." We will refer to her now as OS.

OS told and wrote this story one evening when she and several of her friends were visiting us in our home. They had heard that some boys had made "books" at our house and wanted to do the same. They wanted to tell stories and then write them down to be stapled and then illustrated as the boys had done. This story is presented differently from those read by Rachel. For OS a story was either told face-to-face as an oral performance or it was written, but not both. Recall that for Rachel a story was a read story. OS first told the story and then typed out what she called "the rest." This was a recapitulation of her oral version in type.

The transcription below gives OS's oral version. That is followed by a facsimile of her typed version. In this case slashes indicate rising intonation.

OS'S STORY

OK

.

m

.

GIGGLES

.

OK
um

.

um
(once)
You know what? that time us we were going Doree Lake /

.

and
by the road /

.

us
u-u-us we seen um
um
a bear and two cubs
behind him

.

just climbing up the tree //

.

that tree was just moving like that

.

(Cubs were climbing up the tree?)
Yeah, they were just sitting on top there //

And us we seen a rabbits /

.

and us seen ah

.

and us we seen two squirrels /

.

and um

.

and um

.

and us we going Doree lake, you know /

.

us we
us we
and us we're in the water /

.

us we seen little small baby fish //

.

Just small ones, eh /
GIGGLE
And I'll I'll don't have to tell you the rest
I'll write it
I'll write it down the rest, OK /
(OK)
OK /
OK //

---

on the way   to   Doree Lake   we saw
a bear with to cubs   on a tree
and two   rabbits.

and XXX two squirrels
      in the water we saw   small fishes.
            (OS's name)

The Oral Version

OS's story is characteristic of face-to-face oral performance in spite of the intention to create a written text. It is contextualized and individual. Formulas such as "you know what?" indicate an expectation of listener involvement. Others such as "that time" and "like that" call for an interpretation based on knowledge not contained within the text. In contrast to Rachel's reading prosody this text marks intonation units with rising question intonations that call for audience response. The audience as face-to-face participant is involved in the telling throughout. At the same time the author is not fictionalized. OS refers to herself and her companions as "us we" which parallels the use of the audience address "you know?"

Tone groups are not maintained as strict intonation units. There is much hesitation and recycling. For example there is

and us seen ah

and us we seen two squirrels /

Overall, OS is speaking in a face-to-face situation almost conversationally. We say "almost" because she was aware of the tape recording which she and her friends had initiated. She was nervous about the distance being created by the tape recorder, and we felt it was inconsistent with her conversational or oral orientation in telling the story.

Just at the beginning, as OS was hesitating, another child prompted "Once" in a soft voice. This suggestion that OS place this situation into the traditional written story frame is quickly rejected by OS and even countered with her very conversational opening, "You know what?" OS produces as consistent an oral performance as Rachel produced a literate performance.

A second aspect of OS's oral version is its grammaticality which is "Indian English." this is a further marker of ingroup or informal contextualization. There is "just" as in intensifier as in "that tree was just moving like that." The pronoun "us we" and the use of "him" for an obviously female bear are regular Indian English usages. There is no preposition "to" in the locative "going Doree Lake." Nonagreement of the article "a" and plural "rabbits" further marks this variety as does the verb form "seen" (or in the example below "sawn"). The contraction *we're* may either contract "we were" or "we are." In one case it is contraction of the past tense form, in the other case of the present form which marks this as Indian English. In general we can say that the choice of code is clearly marked and indicative of the nonformal and contextualized nature of the performance.

Finally, the oral version of OS's story compares well with other Athabaskan narration in being formally marked for a four-part narrative structure. In Chipewyan narratives the overall organization is by groups of four. These groups are marked in Chipewyan by the form kú˙ (or ʔɛkú˙) (Scollon 1977) as well as by breathing and pausing (Scollon & Scollon 1979). In English versions the same thing occurs. Forms that are frequently used are "Well," "and," "and then," or "and um." If we look at this story by OS we see that the first boundary is marked by a pitch rise (/), a pause, a breath, and the form "and." This is the initial or orientation to the story.

The second boundary is marked just before OS mentions the rabbits. This boundary has a pitch rise (//), a breath, a pause, and the form "and." This is the end of the first unit or episode.

The third boundary encloses the second episode at the end of that line. Again it is marked with a pitch rise (/), a breath, a pause, and the form "and."

The fourth boundary and third episode are closed again in the same way after mention of the squirrels.

The last boundary that meets these structural criteria of a pitch rise (/), a breath, a pause, and "and" is at the end. It closes out the last and fourth episode, the mention of the small fish. This is followed by the final or closing frame to parallel the initial. She says she will write the rest.

There are two reasons why we have elaborated on OS's marking of the narrative structure. At first glance it is difficult to believe that OS's use of "and" is anything but hesitation or stalling. These markers, however, meet at least two criteria of semanticity. First, they correspond very well functionally to markers of oral narrative structure found in Athabaskan. As such they can be seen as translations of the oral narrative markers. Secondly, the structure of four units they demarcate also corresponds well throughout Athabaskan oral narrative (Scollon & Scollon 1979). The first reason then that we want to elaborate on OS's marking of narrative structure is that it is much more formal than it might appear. This text is squarely within the Athabaskan oral tradition in spite of its being told entirely in English.

The second reason we have gone into this is that this formal structure carries over into the written version below. It is in fact the only aspect that carries over and may thus be considered to be the central feature of OS's story. Her story is contextualized, indexical, conversational, and marked as informal and ingroup but it is nevertheless structurally quite formal. We could point with Rachel to the overriding concern with information structuring and fictionalization of the self. With OS we point to the overriding concern with the abstract formal structuring of the narrative contents. In that sense it is in fact a very abstract performance in spite of its high degree of contextualization.

The Written Version

When OS typed the story she had free use of the typewriter and sufficient paper and time to type at length. She chose instead to present the five-line version already reproduced.

There are several things of interest here. This version is somewhat decontextualized as compared to the oral version. The indicators of contextualization and indexicity such as "you know?" are gone. The information structure is clearer. There are no hesitations or recyclings. But at the same time there is no fictionalization of the author and character as in Rachel's stories. The Indian English "us we" has been replaced by the nearly equally contextualized and nonfictionalized but standard "we."

In another case OS did produce a partly fictionalized account in an oral version. In the selected pieces below though, it can be seen that this fictionalization only applies to others and not the author or OS. Finally, even that fictionalization collapses into second person reference.

There was a girl named A— P—.

.

.

.

She got scared. She went to my house.
She ran to my granny's

.

.

.

and I was babysitting you, you got scared.

Here we can observe the difference between fictionalization and creating fiction. In a story by another child, a six year old, we saw the use of the contextualized pronouns "we" and "my" in a completely fictional context, complete with a formulaic opening.

Once upon a time we sawned a little kid walking around
We sawned a *big town*
My Mommy Cookie was looking for
A big town

It would be better, we think, to consider the written version of OS's story to be more highly formalized but not considerably more decontextualized. It consists of the same four units as the oral version. Here the conventions that mark the units are the ending of a line of type and the use of "and." It should be mentioned that OS left margins and so could have typed a longer line if she had chosen to. The initial is marked only with a new line. The last unit is marked with an indentation and not "and" which is perhaps not a serious inconsistency.

The written version is quite condensed by comparison with the oral version. This does indicate a more compact marshalling of resources consistent with literacy. At the same time it might be said that this brevity is more consistent with the formalization of the oral tradition than with the elaboration and explication of the literate tradition. Hymes (1977) has suggested that a highly succinct version of a traditional narrative may be indicative of narrative control and proficiency. Our own work (Scollon & Scollon 1979) leads us to believe that at Fort Chipewyan this is true. We would suggest that OS's brevity in the written version represents a formalization toward the oral tradition, not toward the written as it might at first suggest.

Finally it can be pointed out that OS's written version is in grammatical "standard" English. There is either one sentence with an implicit conjunction or two sentences, but there is clearly a marked difference between the code in which this version is written and the code of the oral version. This again marks it as formalized and shows the effects of OS's three or so years of schooling.

COMPARING RACHEL AND OS

In order to round out the comparison of these narratives we need to look briefly at the goals they had in telling these stories. OS's general goal and that of her friends on that evening was to equalize herself in terms of favors by competing with the boys who had made "books." Throughout the evening and in other situations there was a strong sense of the social and rhetorical use of storytelling. Stories were used most often to tease others by telling lies about them. Fictionalization of author, audience and character of course would work against that goal. The intention was to put someone in a bad light and enjoy his grief.

Rachel perhaps because she was only two was innocent of such preadolescent motives. Nevertheless in our material there is a clear difference between groups in the functioning of narratives. Narratives were a means of involving the group in an activity. They were a cooperative venture even when the cooperation all worked toward mutual abuse.

A good example of the cooperative functioning of narrative occurred on the way back from a trip to the beach in our car. There was a lot of quarreling about what had happened and how to characterize it. This quarreling was marked by shouting and much simultaneous speech. Then someone said, "M, make it a story." This girl, a ten year old, began to say what had happened. She formalized it with a traditional Athabaskan initial and closed it with a traditional Athabaskan final, all in English. As she told her story the others all listened and chimed in their support and additional details.

For Rachel, we have said, stories were written and read. They were used to produce formal, carefully structured displays in which Rachel as author, audience, and often as character were given distance from each other. They were willingly tape recorded.

We reach the irony of saying that Rachel, although she could not read or write, was on her way to literacy. Her English was ungrammatical and immature but she was literate in a more general sense. OS, on the other hand, could read, write, and type and yet in an important sense was not as literate as Rachel. Her written version was highly grammatical but, we feel, deeply oral and non-literate in its orientation.

The Literate Orientation

To this point we have looked at the reading and writing of stories by Rachel and OS. We have argued that by contrast with OS, Rachel before her third birthday was literate in her orientation to stories. Now we would like to look at a number of other ways in which Rachel showed her orientation to literacy.

Mixed throughout her conversation were allusions to things she had read, that is, to things she had heard read. They often made no sense in terms of the ongoing situation but appeared as decontextualized signs of her developing literacy. We heard such things as "have no fear" and "full of happiness" which Rachel could trace directly to their literary source, even if we could not.

As we have mentioned above, Rachel sang the "ABC" song, had a set of alphabet blocks and her own books. She often made up rhymes on models she got out of written sources such as

> Apple skin
> Apple skin
> Apple skin's red
> Apple skin
> Apple skin
> Apple skin's red

or

> Hunk
> Hunk
> Your nose smells like punk.

Decontextualization Through the Manipulation of Contexts

Rachel played not only with the sounds of words but with the grammatical relationships among them. Punning can be thought of as decontextualization through double contextualization. By placing a word in several contexts simultaneously one achieves a third effect. Rachel not only punned but could find ways to speak about the consciousness of punning.

Once when she was two years and five months old she said pointing to letters in her book, "This is a 'P' and this is a little 'p'." When her father said there was more pee in her potty she looked puzzled and then as she understood said "You surprised me." She paused and then said, "I turned off the light and I was surprised." This latter comment was a reference to the time she had wanted to see what the light switch would do. When she turned it off and was plunged into darkness she had been delighted and surprised. Now she was saying that the relationship of "P," "p," and "pee" was like throwing a light switch and being plunged into darkness by surprise.

In another case Rachel said, "There's two kind of 'o' [oú] and [oú]." When her father wrote the letter "O" she said it was [oú]. The other she indicated intonationally was the "Oh!" of surprise.

She showed explicit knowledge of paradigmatic relationships among words. Once she was going around with a book asking someone to read. She said, "I want this to be read. I want this to be read." Her mother said, "It can't be red, it's orange." Rachel answered, "I said *read, read* [rɛd]." Her mother repeated, teasing her, "It can't be red, it's orange." Rachel said, "No, *read* [rɛd]. I said *read* [rid] a different way." This example shows that she sees the relationship between *read* (present) and *read* (past) as saying the *same thing* a different way. She would not have actually known, we believe, that the spellings are identical. She was able, though, to find an expression for the paradigmatic relationship of present and past tense forms. We feel that this bespeaks the literate orientation toward grammaticality.

Rachel's ability to manipulate verbal contexts indicates a control over contexts which is essential to the decontextualization of literacy. Once we had this conversation:

Rachel: I heard the fire when I was outside.

Mother: You heard the siren!

Rachel: I heard the fire when I was outside.

Father: What did the fire sound like?

Rachel: I sounded like "tire."

Both as an indication of verbal play and an ability to dodge, this example shows her ability to control talk by controlling contexts.

As a final example, at Fort Chipewyan the Chipewyan word *ma* "it stinks" has been appropriated by everyone in the community as an interjection to indicate surprise, interest, or disapproval. A further detail that is needed to interpret this example is that there is a newspaper called *The Moccasin Telegram*. One time after a scolding Rachel said "Ma" and just as her father was about to respond to this direct contradiction of parental authority she added "casin Telegram." The shift of contexts of course was funny enough to end the scolding in laughter.

The Fictionalization of Self in Global Statements

Through her manipulation of the sounds and grammatical forms of language Rachel showed a strong orientation to the decontextualization and high information levels required for literacy. At the same time she showed an orientation to the fictionalization of self that is an essential ingredient of the authorship and readership roles. This orientation showed up in a whole range of global statements Rachel began to make in this period.

As an example of what we mean by a global statement we can look at the time her father asked her to bring the vacuum cleaner. First Rachel tried to pick it up with one hand. When that didn't work her father suggested she pick it up with both hands. When she failed at that she said, "It can't work if little kids use both hands." Here as in her stories she characterizes herself in the third person. She goes even further in referring to herself by the class of which she is a member, the class of "little kids." It is not herself or even Rachel that is having difficulty. All little kids are implicated in Rachel's statement.

Another similar case occurred when Rachel passed a girl about her age walking home one day. They waved at each other and then she said, "When kids are outside all the other kids are supposed to wave their hands who are outside too." Beyond the preoccupation with social behavior we can see again the global statement. Rachel subsumes her own activity to the activity of the role, the little kid who is outside.

Along with these we can see the same global statement in "Most people don't use soap when they shave." To the question of how many people she had watched shave she answered, "Just you, Daddy." But it is not simply a case of generalizing the behavior of her own family to the rest of the world. Rachel also said when we had oatmeal for breakfast, "Most of the people don't have oatmeal." We feel that these statements which show an interest in viewing the world in terms of categories rather than individuals are consonant with the fictionalization of the roles of author, audience, and character in Rachel's stories.

Her ability to create narrative roles was virtually unlimited. Once she said while watching her father chop an onion, "Chuck, chuck, chuck. That's what the knife said to the onion." In her literate world the self can be removed to the third person or knives and onions can engage in dialogue. The freedom of movement of these characters is typical of the decontextualization of the literate orientation.

Teaching the Literate Orientation

The essayist style of literacy can be generally characterized as decontextualized language. There are two areas of decontextualization that we have suggested are central, the creation of an explicit, grammatically and lexically marked information structure which is high in new information, and the fictionalization of the roles of author, audience, and in autobiography of the self. We have presented evidence that before she had reached her third birthday Rachel had made major advances toward control of the essayist orientation. By contrast with other children at Fort Chipewyan, Rachel could be seen as developing in a very different way. We would like to suggest that Rachel's career as a two year old literate was part of an ongoing socialization to literacy, that from much earlier we as her parents had given quite explicit instruction in this orientation to literacy.

RAISING THE PERCENTAGE
OF NEW INFORMATION

When we began our study of Rachel's language development in 1974 we had in mind a study which would give us a view on a child's language in the first year. R. Scollon's study of a one year old (Scollon 1976) had led us to believe that much before the onset of two-word constructions there were important developments that arose out of discourse interactions. The vertical construction was seen as the forerunner of the two-word construction, as the foundation on which syntax is built.

What is important about the vertical construction is that it develops in interactions with other speakers, usually the caregivers. A typical early vertical construction is as follows (Scollon 1976):

> B: Kimby
> Mother: What about Kimby?
> B: Close.

The child says something. The mother asks what about it and the child says something further. The first can be seen as a topic statement, the mother's comment as a request for a comment and the child's answer as giving the comment.

As the child develops she begins to take over both roles. That is, Brenda soon began to say both the topic and the comment. As soon as these became prosodically linked as a single utterance the whole process shifted up a level. The whole topic-comment pair was taken as given and the interlocutor sought another comment. An example of one of these more elaborate pairs is as follows:

> B: Tape recorder
>   use it
>   use it
> Int: Use it for what?
> B: talk
>   corder talk
>   Brenda talk

Two things are important for this discussion. One is that this development is based on interaction with other speakers. The other is that it involves the progressive incorporation within a single tone group of greater amounts of new information.

As we began our study of Rachel's early development we began to be aware that the vertical construction was not essential to syntactic development in English. Bloom (1973) had observed the same phenomenon but had felt that these early constructions were not syntactic. At the same time the work of Peters (1977, 1978) had convinced us that children with very different learning strategies were achieving essentially the same structural goals. Nelson (1975) had pointed out important differences in referentiality among children and further pointed out that what appeared to be significant was the matching between child and caregivers on strategies.

In our work with Rachel by the second year we had seen virtually the same development that had been described for Brenda (Scollon 1976). It was of such little interest that we felt we had nothing new. Only when Rachel's development was seen in contrast to the children at Fort Chipewyan did her language as well as Brenda's appear in the relief necessary to see vertical construction as an important preparation for literacy rather than for syntax.

The important concept here is that the vertical construction is an interactive mechanism by which the caregiver calls for a continual upgrading of the new information content. The syntactic development that accompanies this process is independent to a considerable extent. The vertical construction is a discourse process as is the information structuring of essayist literacy. We now see the former as an important means of teaching the latter.

NARRATIVE ACCOUNTING

In the quotation used earlier Hall (1973) has said that we are all engaged in authoring our autobiographies. As we began to review our notes over the period preceding our arrival at Fort Chip ewyan we began to see that in this area as well we had given Rachel quite explicit instruction in the authorship of her autobiography. As an example of how Rachel learned to place herself in the third person role of central character in a story we can describe our ride into Edmonton. It was a long day of driving. Rachel at two years and two months was tired and fussy. We planned to clean up from our camping trip in Edmonton and enjoy a meal in a restaurant. It was essential for Rachel to sleep for all this to happen.

We began telling her stories in the format of traditional stories but with her as the main character and Edmonton and that evening as the setting. A paraphrase of the beginning of one would be,

> "Once upon a time there was a little girl named Rachel. She was real tired from camping and riding in the car. She fell asleep while her Daddy held her. When she woke up they were in Edmonton. They went to a motel, got cleaned up and went out for supper and had a nice time."

These stories set up a pleasant future in which it was not only safe but desirable to go to sleep and they had the effect of lulling her to sleep. The point here is that they provided a clear model for the distancing of ourselves from the situation through a narrative about the situation.

Much earlier, three days after her first birthday, we had recorded a full day of Rachel's waking activity. In going over this material we had been puzzled by an aspect of the baby talk register for which we had not been able to account. We had noticed that we had done a lot of coaching of narration. At one year of age Rachel could not speak, of course, and it struck us as strange that we should have devoted so much energy to seeking these self-accountings.

As an example we can look at a moment early in the day when Rachel fell and bumped her head. As she cried her father said,

> Aw, yeah.
> Here. Here. You bumped your head.
> Oh, baby.
> Aw-aw-poor kid.
> N,n,n,n.
> What tripped you? Did you see what tripped you?

As she continues crying, her mother says,

> Nothing tripped her, just lost her balance.

This comment is marked by high pitch, light voice, and a sing-song intonation. That is, it is not a direct refutation of the father's account. It is in the baby talk register as an alternative account rendered in the third person.

We can see in this example that Rachel's father suggests that her crying is inappropriate unless explained. He further suggests a narrative account for this "flooding out." The mother does not agree with the attribution of blame but does agree that it is appropriate for Rachel to account for her current behavior with a narrative account, however brief. This is the background against which Rachel first began to speak.

As another example a bit later in the same day in playing catch Rachel managed to catch the ball. Her father says, "Yeah, you caught it." As the play goes on he gives a running account of the activity.

> Oh, you threw it all the way to Mommy.
> Here throw it to me.

See, that's how we do it.

That's how we do.

See, look.

We throw it up and catch it.

We throw it up and catch it.

Up—and catch it.

It goes up—and I catch it.

Up and I catch it.

This example not only gives a play-by-play account, it phrases it in the same global terms that Rachel another year or so later learns to use herself. We throw it. We catch it.

It is striking that looking back now at the material on Brenda we can see much of the same narrative accounting. In an instance quoted elsewhere (Scollon 1976) we have,

Brenda

sleeping

> Hm? Yeah, you thought lady was wearing blanket, didn't you?

bus

bus

> Yeah, on the bus, hm?

The narrative that Brenda gives and the one given by her mother do not agree. Brenda is speaking of falling asleep in the bus. Her mother is speaking of Brenda's mistaking a woman's skirt for her sister's blanket because they were made of the same material. This happened in the doctor's office and caused the mother some embarrassment.

Brenda is constructing a minimal narrative account of her own in this case. The mother, however, is taking that occasion to present another narrative for Brenda. Although it disagrees in this case with what Brenda is saying, it is phrased as "you thought," not "she thought." that is, the mother is speaking for Brenda. It seems that one of the mother's interests here is to demonstrate to Brenda how she may account for her behavior in the doctor's office.

We can see in these examples that in this coaching of narrative accounts during the first year and second year there is a mechanism for fostering the literate orientation of taking distance from oneself.

It is as natural for a literate parent to do this as it is for her to coach her infant in the decontextualization of authorship. We suggest then that in this component of the baby talk register there is important foundation work being done in the preparation for literacy.

As a last comment on the naturalness of teaching of the literate orientation we can mention Rachel's answer to her father's question. He asked, "Who taught you to write stories?" She answered, "Nobody. I learned it myself."

PREPARATION FOR LITERACY

Cook-Gumperz (1978) has suggested that typical interactive styles in schooling serve as preparation for literacy. She argues that features such as teachers calling for close attention before giving verbal instructions highlight the child's focus upon the purely linguistic aspects of the message. This prepares the way for literacy which as we have already suggested requires heightened attention to several aspects of the linguistic code. As Cook-Gumperz argues, this increased dependence on the linguistic code actually is unproductive for children at first and places the teacher in a double-bind situation. The teacher must insist on a type of decontextualization that in the ongoing school life is less useful than the highly contextualized peer-style interaction.

One detail which Cook-Gumperz notes that is of interest by comparison with Foucault's work (mentioned in the preceding chapter) is the teacher's insistence that good posture is an essential aspect of paying attention. Foucault (1977b) has argued that the military review is intimately related to the general reorganization of knowledge that produced the essayist prose style. In the same way that the author as person is fully effaced in the essay, the soldier as person is fully effaced in the military review as is the child as person in the school exam. What is presented to the ruling gaze is a pure representation of internalized rational knowledge.

We have taken Cook-Gumperz's idea a little further and suggested several ways in which patterns of linguistic socialization in the child's life before school are continuous with the school preparation for literacy in many segments of western society. Our argument has been that there were important differences between our daughter Rachel and other children at Fort Chipewyan in their orientation to literacy. Before her third birthday Rachel had shown that for her literacy was located or typified very much in the same way it was for us. She had developed important skills in decontextualization both of information structure and of the authorship role. By contrast the children of Fort Chipewyan were oriented toward a Qur'anic typification of literacy. For them it was inappropriate. Their own literate productions were oriented toward the traditional and oral.

We have also argued that these orientations are the result of specific patterns of socialization. In the case of Rachel we have the material to suggest a careful program of coaching in literacy from early in life. The orientation that we have described for Rachel at two we see as the outcome of this program of unconscious parental instruction in literacy.

This argument has implications for research in literacy and education. If, as we have argued, Rachel's literate orientation is the product of a program of socialization for literacy, then it would be possible to treat this as a hypothesis for comparative and longitudinal research. We should expect a correlation between parental or caregiver patterns of instruction in the first two years and literacy skills in the school years. We should expect two year olds like Rachel to have little to learn about literacy but the mechanics of spelling and conventions of elegant visual display in the early school years. We should expect children from other orientations to find it difficult to develop the literate orientation in spite of heavy teaching of grammar, spelling, conventions of presentation, and oral display of reading ability.

We would like to advance a caution here. In the preceding chapter we have argued that the discourse patterns of essayist literacy, the patterns that we have described here as Rachel's orientation to literacy, are highly consonant with the discourse patterns of a particular ethnic group, our "English speakers." At least for Athabaskans, essayist literacy is experienced as interethnic communication and suffers from much of the ethnic stereotyping that confounds Athabaskan–English interethnic communication. We suggest that Rachel's orientation to literacy is not simply an orientation to literacy but in addition it is to a large extent an orientation to the discourse patterns of English-speaking educated middle class Americans and Canadians. The orientation of the children at Fort Chipewyan by the same token is not only an orientation to traditional Athabaskan oral narrative, it is an orientation to patterns of Athabaskan discourse. As we consider possible hypotheses about literacy and education that might be suggested by our arguments here we want to be careful to understand that these hypotheses are also very likely to be hypotheses about ethnicity and changes in ethnicity. We can no longer assume that essayist literacy is or should be the goal of all education any more than we would assume that all school children should be ethnically identified with any one dominant ethnic group.

FIVE

THE BUSH CONSCIOUSNESS AND ORAL NARRATIVE DISCOURSE

A PROBLEM OF DESCRIPTION

The discussion of world-view is always difficult even where the reality set being described is that of both the author and the reader. In the case of the modern consciousness and essayist literacy, the goal of description is simplified considerably by the fact that the very text in which the description is made exemplifies the same orientation. In the case of the bush consciousness, however, we run into a descriptive problem. The bush consciousness must be assumed to be largely unfamiliar to most readers. Furthermore, in significant ways this reality set contrasts with the essayist presentational format in which it is being described. The description tends to undermine itself at every point.

Perhaps the most serious problem, though, comes from the contrast between the bush consciousness we are describing and the modern consciousness of the reader we assume. There is a tendency for the properties we describe for the bush consciousness to be perceived as negative qualities in any phrasing we may choose because they directly negate structural properties of the modern consciousness. We ask the reader to approach this discussion of the bush consciousness as openly as possible. It is our hope that in concluding this chapter with a discussion of oral narrative we will be able in part to exemplify the properties that we outline here and in doing so give the reader at least some sense of the internal consistency and high viability of the bush consciousness.

THE FOUR ASPECTS OF
THE BUSH CONSCIOUSNESS

In our work at Fort Chipewyan (Scollon & Scollon 1979) we characterized a reality set which we called the bush consciousness. As we have argued for the modern consciousness, this reality set is not truly isomorphous with any cultural, social, or ethnic group. On the basis of our experience at Fort Chipewyan and on reading the ethnographic literature we felt that this reality set was characteristic, however, of a predominant group of native (and some non-native) northern Canadians and Alaskans. We are relating it more closely than we did in the past to Northern Athabaskans in this discussion. Again, though, we should caution that it is just one possibility that is not wholly characteristic of all Athabaskans.

Individual Respect

The central aspect of the bush consciousness is respect for the individual. There is a widely held feeling that this can be easily accounted for by the living conditions under which northern Athabaskans have remained a viable social group. Because of the scarcity of game and the extreme distances that must be covered, sometimes during very cold weather, material culture developments have been kept to a minimum. Social and cognitive elaboration have had to be quite literally portable. The single individual as a viable unit of survival under extreme duress has been the most adaptive mode of social development. Athabaskans have chosen to rely heavily on the development of the knowledge, skills, and adaptive flexibility of each separate individual as the central means of group survival. The bush consciousness, then, centers around the knowledge and needs of this individual.

Nonintervention

Because of the high respect paid to the individual in the bush consciousness, it is important for all to be careful not to intervene in his activities, thinking and movements. There is a reluctance to interfere with others and by extension a reluctance to interfere with nature, luck, or the future. The self-respect of the individual is mutually regarded by all as inviolable and protected through nonintervention.

This aspect of the bush consciousness becomes its learning mode. While the experience of the individual is considered his own best teacher, it is felt that those with the greatest experience must be valued for that experience. Individuals seek out others with greater experience to learn from them in anticipation of their own needs. Children are told to listen when elders speak, partly out of respect for age and nonintervention, but more importantly because that is how one prepares for one's own experience. Attention rather than silence is fostered. Attention to the natural world is equally fostered. Children are expected constantly to observe the world about them and to learn from it.

From this it can be seen that one does not "teach" a child or a learner. This amount of intervention in the child's autonomy would risk forever destroying the child's ability to observe and learn for his own motives. The child is encouraged only to seek out knowledge of human experience and skills by being present in the practice or their telling. It is said that it is a wise and fortunate child who has his grandparents "in his ear." A child who has overheard his grandparents and their peers speak of the world is best equipped for his own life.

Integration of Knowledge

From the need of the individual to develop an autonomous view of his own experience comes the importance of nonintervention in his life and learning. We characterize the knowledge of the individual as highly integrated. Whatever is known is known from the point of view of the individual. Knowledge that is not relevant to the needs of the individual is seen as at least problematical if it is not completely rejected. What is of importance in any knowledge is that the individual can see how to incorporate it into his own experience. Knowledge that is not integrated may prove useless under the stressful conditions of survival assumed for the individual. The bush consciousness then tends to reject expertise that other individuals may have unless one can see a way to incorporate that knowledge into his own knowledge structures. The goal is a holistic, internally consistent known world-view or reality set.

Entropy

The fourth aspect is the most difficult about which to write. Because of the emphasis on the individual and the need for the individual to internally integrate his own knowledge, there is a tendency to reject outside knowledge or other influences that cannot be easily integrated into the individual's view of the world. The higher order structures that are organized to integrate very different or essentially irreconcilable events and views are rejected by the bush consciousness in favor of lower order structures. We have used the term "entropy" to suggest this preference for lower order structures over high order structures. Because the modern consciousness in its componentiality and extreme pluralism values the successive development of higher and higher order structures it is difficult to give convincing examples of this entropic aspect of the bush consciousness which do not appear quite negative to the modern consciousness.

When the two reality sets are in contact this aspect tends to produce a conflict in values that to the modern consciousness appears as the positive love of disorder. The "disorder" and "unruliness" that the modern consciousness perceives in the bush consciousness are, we feel, a result of this aspect of the bush consciousness. It only becomes a negative aspect in the view of the modern consciousness. For the bush consciousness it is positive and consistent with the need for deep respect of the individual.

CONTRASTS WITH THE
MODERN CONSCIOUSNESS

We have now seen that there is at least the potential for conflict between the entropic aspect of the bush consciousness and the componentiality and pluralism of the modern consciousness. The systematicity of the modern consciousness is often felt as unnatural and threatening to the bush consciousness and so rejected or at least avoided. The bureaucratic and technological institutions of the modern consciousness tend to proliferate system and organization, which, because of the high respect for the individual of the bush consciousness, threaten the autonomy of the individual.

Individuality

In discussing the individual aspect of the bush consciousness we have sometimes encountered the objection that after all, Americans and Canadians are also highly individualistic. We have a problem of wording, then, which we would like to clarify. The individual of the bush consciousness is assumed to be a viable unit of survival under extremes of isolation and environmental duress. Literally we mean a person should be able to feed, house, and clothe himself for perhaps months with nothing but what he can carry himself in deep snow at perhaps $-40°$. While this extreme is perhaps not often encountered in the life of the individual, the preparation is still assumed and perhaps more importantly, it is assumed that the individual will possess the mental characteristics that would allow him to survive as a healthy, normal member of society under such conditions.

The individuality of the modern consciousness is a very different thing. It is the individuality of the component. We believe that what is experienced by the modern consciousness as individuality is a boundedness, an isolability, and an interchangeability. One is distinct, perhaps, from all others, but not by any means independent. Each (individual) component is a part of a large system on which it crucially depends for survival as well as self-definition. We would argue that while we seem to be forced to use the same term, "individuality," for both cases, the bush consciousness individual is a very different phenomenon from the modern consciousness individual. The bush consciousness individual knows an autonomy and self-containment that is perhaps characteristic only of whole social groups for the modern consciousness.

Nonintervention

As we have said in regard to the individual in the modern consciousness, it is the individuality of the component of a larger system. From this comes the distinct preference of the modern consciousness for the rule of the system, the rule of the law, over the rule of the individual. Individual freedom is freedom to move within a role or position, or freedom to be exchanged in another position with an equivalent component. The bush consciousness, on the other hand, emphasizes the autonomy of the individual. In this light nonintervention or mutual respect for the individuality of others is an essential element of system stability. Without reciprocal nonintervention there would be no larger system. The potential runaway autonomy of individuals is held in check by the mutual respect of others which is held in equally high regard. We have then the seeming paradox that for the bush consciousness the autonomy of the individual can only be achieved to the extent that it is granted to one by others. Individual autonomy is, in fact, a social product. One gains autonomy to the extent one grants it. This negotiation, however, is always conducted on the basis of individuals. Each person in each situation is constrained only by his own wish to be granted autonomy. Even in this the autonomy of the individual is preserved. One respects others as one's own choice motivated by one's own wish for mutual respect.

Integration

The modern consciousness views knowledge as essentially limitless and continually expanding. It assumes that no individual can know all that is knowable and thus we have experts and specialists and the systems which index this specialization of knowledge. Individual knowledge for the modern consciousness is seen as being best developed in the indexing system. It is seen as more productive to know how to use a dictionary than to know all of the words in a language.

The bush consciousness, on the other hand, being constrained historically by limits on what could be carried and by relatively infrequent meetings with other groups, emphasizes the integration of knowledge into one's own needs. What has become highly developed is the ability to integrate information into a whole and coherent view of the world. This integrative ability appears to the modern consciousness as phenomenal memory ability and as an ability to make "intuitive leaps." It also appears as a considerable parsimony of expression. As we will discuss below, the metonymical abstraction of themes organizes knowledge and expression. This parsimony often strikes the modern consciousness as highly cryptic if not wholly unintelligible. By the same token, the backgrounding and indexing of knowledge of the modern consciousness strikes the bush consciousness as dealing in structures of irrelevance.

THE EXPRESSIVE MEANS OF THE
BUSH CONSCIOUSNESS: ORAL NARRATIVE

For the bush consciousness the primary means of acquiring knowledge are personal experience and stories of the experiences of others. Perhaps now we can see why this should be so. In the first place, it is essential for knowledge to be contextualized in the experience of individuals. Knowledge for its own sake is rejected. At the same time, knowledge that was passed on by moral, ethical, or even pragmatic authority and rule would too strongly threaten the autonomy of the individual learner. Authoritarian knowledge could not be counted on to account for every new experience in the highly unpredictable natural world and survival might require a quick readjustment to new conditions. Knowledge must be passed on in such a way that it maximizes relevance to the learner and minimizes the threat to his individual autonomy and flexibility.

Oral narrative presents just such a teaching and learning mechanism, as we will try to show. As narrative it is deeply contextualized in the experience of the teller for personal histories and in the experience of the ancestors in more traditional genres. For the learner knowledge is presented in a take-it-or-leave-it manner that reflects a respect for his independence. It is entirely up to the learner what he makes of it. It is the storyteller's art to anticipate carefully the future needs of the listener as well as his current knowledge and predisposition. As with nonintervention, the storyteller to protect his own autonomy characterizes his knowledge as being only his own experience while being deeply concerned about the receptive possibilities of his audience. An understanding of oral narrative as performance directed to the needs of the audience is essential to our understanding of the bush consciousness.

A Poetics of Oral Narrative

It is now more than twenty years since Jacobs first argued for the importance of seeing American Indian oral narratives as something more akin to dramatic poetry in the western tradition than to the essayist prose into which they had so often been translated (Jacobs 1959). It was his point that translations of American Indian oral narratives must be sensitive to generic constraints as well as to phonological and morphological considerations. Now

105

twenty years later we are beginning to see a poetics of oral performance emerging in a body of work encompassing folklore, linguistics, and anthropology, and merging to some extent with the work of modern western poets in the ethnopoetics tradition.

Ten years ago Toelken pointed out the importance of viewing Navajo Coyote narratives in the contexts of their performance. Others such as Hymes (1971, 1975a, 1975b, 1976, 1977, 1978, 1979), Tedlock (1972a, 1972b, 1973, 1975, 1976), Dauenhauer (1975, 1976a), and Foster (1974) have shown the importance of treating the style and form of the original text in performance as a significant carrier of meaning. It is now clear that narrative texts in these traditions are carefully structured. Words that were once treated as repetitious and tiresome such as might be translated with "and" or "and then" are now known to be crucial to the narrative organization.

Hymes (1977) has suggested that we use terms such as "line," "verse," and "stanza" in speaking of this narrative organization as a way of reminding ourselves that these narratives more closely parallel our own poetic traditions than those of our prose style as might be suggested by terms such as "paragraph." In our own work beginning with Chipewyan and now involving other Athabaskan languages, we have seen the same generic definition and precision (Scollon 1976b, 1976c, 1977, 1979a, 1979b, to appear, Scollon & Scollon 1979). It is this generic structure which is so critical in the expression of the bush consciousness to which we now turn.

TRANSLATION SETS

A problem in the study of narrative structure is to find some source of verification of the analysis. There are at least four possible sources. The first is the internal logic of the analysis. This is the Aristotelian logic of the three parts, the beginning, the middle, and the end. A story which is overtly marked as having three sections and which at least tolerates if not encourages an analysis into the Aristotelian logic is perceived as ringing true to some logic external to the events narrated. It is this "ringing true" that verifies the analysis. Unfortunately, when working outside our own tradition the true ring of an analysis is dangerously suspect.

In some cases an analysis of narrative structure may be supported by independent ethnographic or stylistic studies. In an earlier study of a Chipewyan text, R. Scollon (1977) found that just where the analysis required a division into separate episodes, an independent ethnographic account pointed to a considerable passage of time. The only marker of this time and event change was in fact the boundary between episodes.

Such strokes of good fortune are not so common, however, and we have sought in much of our work to use what we regard as a much more reliable source of verification. In translation sets a narrator tells a story first in one language and then in another. This situation has arisen quite naturally in our work where we have elicited texts in Athabaskan. The narrators have been concerned that we would not understand the Athabaskan version and have retold the whole story in English for our benefit. A comparison of the texts told under these conditions shows a striking parallelism. In some cases the English version reads like a line-by-line translation of the Athabaskan version (Scollon & Scollon 1979). The units marked in each version correspond very directly. Furthermore, the fact that what is marked morphologically in one language may be marked intonationally in the other precludes any suggestion that one text constitutes a simple word-by-word translation, particularly since these texts are told as wholes from beginning to end without break or open reference to the other text. Each text is created anew from the underlying themes and the parallels are the product, we argue, of important principles of the organization of genres.

Beyond the internal logic of the analysis, independent ethnographic studies, and translation sets, the most reliable source of verification of the analysis is the informed judgment of the native critic. In the most recent work on which this study is based we have worked together with Eliza Jones of the Alaska Native Language Center in translating and analyzing personal history narratives in Koyukon Athabaskan told by her uncle Chief Henry of Huslia. These stories were not elicited for text analysis as the preceding texts had been but were recorded with the intention of speaking to future generations.

The analysis we report here of Athabaskan narratives is based on studies of Chipewyan texts (Li & Scollon 1976) as dictated to a linguist, Chipewyan translation sets recorded on audio tape with a live audience, Chipewyan radio broadcasts, Tanacross translation sets, and Koyukon oral histories. Some of the English narratives come from the translation sets just mentioned. The others were tape recorded in live performances by elders whose first languages include most of the Athabaskan languages of Alaska. In our analysis we have relied considerably on the work of Jones and her analysis of the Koyukon texts. The striking parallels in all versions, whether in Athabaskan or English, speak to the depth of the principles of the organization of the oral narrative we are outlining here.

LINE, VERSE, STANZA, AND SCENE

The line in Athabaskan narratives is all that is said between pauses. This line may be as short as a single monosyllabic word or as long as several sentences. A very long line will include a breath taken quickly without a pause in rare cases. A normal line is somewhat less than a full sentence and will consist of several words.

The line is the unit which paces the narrative. Where explanation is highlighted, lines are long and spoken rapidly. As the narrative action increases, lines tend to shorten and the pace is slowed. The line is the rhythmic heart of the narrative performance.

The verse is the result of the interaction of pausing and the grammar. The verse is begun as a new sentence. If the sentence is still incomplete at the end of the line, the next line continues the verse. The verse ends where the end of a line coincides with the close of a sentence. If a sentence should close at a pause which the narrator does not wish to have heard as verse final, a morpheme of continuation is used (e.g. Chipewyan –ú, xéɬ, Tanacross –ts'í', áɬ, Koyukon ts'ʉh, yiɬ).

A verse then begins with the closure of the preceding verse. It ends where there is grammatical closure and a pause. It consists of at least a single clause and a single line.

In English narratives spoken by Athabaskans in this style the verse is marked in the same way with one exception. Intonation is used to signal either continuation or closure. Where a line is intended to continue the verse, it is held on a non-falling, non-final pitch. Where the pitch falls at a grammatical closure and a pause, the verse is ended. In this case then we see non-final intonation at the end of a line in English as translating the Athabaskan continuation morphemes.

Stanzas consist of at least a single verse. They are indicated by a group of markers which amount to a summation of other markers. The most important stanza markers are grammatical closure of the preceding stanza and verse, falling intonation at the preceding closure, a pause, and a lexical marker. These lexical markers may be quite varied and individual narrators often show their own preferences. In the Koyukon of Chief Henry we have the markers shown in Table 2, all within a single extended story. In each case the marker appears as a line by itself forming a clear demarcation of stanzas.

Table 2
Stanza Markers in Koyukon Stories of Chief Henry

Ts'ʉh	At'eey ło
Ts'ʉhʉ	Ts'a yoogh
Ts'a hałda	Ts'ʉh yoogh
Ts'ʉh go	Ts'a go
Ts'ʉh eeyit	Hʉyił hʉn
Kk'ʉdaa	Go hʉn
Eeyit	Hʉyił go yoogh
Eeyit hałda	Hʉyił go
Eeyit hał	Hʉyił go hʉn
Go hałda	Hu ło ts'a
Hałda tł'ogho	Ło ts'a
Doggone	Ts'ʉh ahʉ
My	Eeyit go hʉn
Doo'	Ts'ʉh go hʉn
Ts'ʉh kk'ʉdaa	Kk'ʉdaa go
Ts'ʉh kk'ʉdaa yoogh	Kk'ʉdaa tł'eegho yoogh

In the Tanacross narratives of Gaither Paul there are the markers given in Table 3.

Table 3
Stanza Markers in Tanacross Stories of Gaither Paul

aiy áł	ts'í'
aiy tł'áann	k'ód nitháat
dée'	k'ód aiy áł
k'ód	k'ód áł

Gaither Paul does not, however, use all of these in any one story, and in some cases uses just one throughout a single story.

In Chipewyan, again, there are a variety of markers, as in Table 4.

Table 4
Stanza Markers in Chipewyan Stories

ʔɛkúˑ	kúˑ
kúˑ ʔɛyɛr	kúˑ hų́łdų́ˑ
kų́łdų́ˑ	ʔɛyɛr hots'į̀

Francois Mandeville, the storyteller recorded by Li (Li & Scollon 1976) was highly parsimonious in his use of verse and stanza markers, using only ʔɛkúˑfor stanzas and kúˑfor verses. R. Scollon has argued elsewhere (Scollon 1979a) that this is a further reflection of Mandeville's concern with creating a highly polished literate style.

English narratives in the Athabaskan style mark stanzas with "and," "and then," "but," and "so." Most often these words are set on a separate line to indicate their status as formal markers. It is an unfortunate result of this formality of presentation that some English speakers hear these as hesitations and regard them as reflecting the incompetence of the narrator. On the contrary, they demonstrate a high degree of competence with marking the narrative structure.

Finally, the scene is very Aristotelian. It is the largest unit of organization in the narrative. The scene is determined primarily on the basis of a change of location, a major change of time or season, or a change of the major participants or their activities. The scene boundary coincides with a stanza boundary and may not be otherwise marked.

While shorter narratives may consist of only one scene, probably none extend beyond four scenes. The pattern number in Athabaskan is four. Jacobs (1959) suggested that the organization of the contents or motifs of a narrative may not be in groups of threes as in European folklore. Clackamas Chinook tales he observed to organize around fours and fives. Toelken (1969) pointed out the importance of four in Navajo narratives and Witherspoon (1977) has recently reiterated this importance. Kintsch (1977, Kintsch & Greene 1978) has suggested that memory of stories may be affected by schemata of organization that are culturally-based. His subjects, University of Colorado students, tended to reduce four-part Athabaskan stories to three parts either by forgetting one part or by collapsing two into one to produce a total of three. We suggest that scenes in narratives are most reflective of the Athabaskan pattern number four. Kintsch's work suggests that the organization of memory may be closely related to the organization of scenes in narratives.

STANZAS AND PERSPECTIVE

The function of the stanza is to mark perspective. At the beginning of each stanza a new point of view is taken. This idea of point of view is a bit elusive in some cases but nevertheless it seems the best way to speak generally of the stanza. As an example of stanza perspective, in Chipewyan anaphoric pronominal references (ʔɛyi or bɛ) may not cross stanza boundaries (Scollon 1977). In Tanacross, however, the cognate anaphoric free pronoun (aiy) is used for just this function of crossing stanza boundaries in anaphoric references. Within a stanza in Tanacross non-pronominal anaphoric reference is to the first mentioned subject noun phrase.

The focused participant within a stanza, the first mentioned participant, may be defocused or another participant temporarily focused. This sort of temporary refocusing within the stanza is accomplished by the separate system of so-called subject-object inversion (Thompson 1979). Generally, however, it remains true that the stanza is the unit of perspective governing anaphoric reference.

Besides the introduction and shift of focal participants the stanza indicates other shifts in perspective. Changes in the time framing of events occasion new stanzas. A storyteller saying "I went to bed" and "I got up" places these in separate stanzas if not in separate scenes if each is regarded as a separate unit of the narrative. A new action or major shift in the flow of the narrative is marked by a new stanza. A shift in aspect such as that between returning home and arriving there is placed in separate stanzas.

Another category of narrative marked by stanzas is commentary that is removed from the backbone of the narrative action. Comments and evaluative statements are placed in separate stanzas. Statements of intentions and plans or general statements about the nature of the world are given separate stanzas. Finally, comments on inferred reality are separated from narrative of observed reality in different stanzas.

We continue to use the term "perspective" to cover the various kinds of material contained in stanzas even though we mean to include much beyond the focusing of participants. The function of the stanza is to show where some departure from expectation is taking place. These departures from expectation may have to do with narrative characters, actions, events or the narrative event itself with backbone distinguished from evaluation and commentary.

VERSES AND GROUNDING

The function of the verse is to indicate grounding. We may build on Hopper and Thompson's (to appear) definition of grounding.

> That part of a discourse which does not immediately and crucially contribute to the speaker's goal, but which merely assists, amplifies, or comments on it, is referred to as BACKGROUND. By contrast, the material which supplies the main points of the discourse is known as FOREGROUND: Linguistic features associated with the distinction between foreground and background are referred to as GROUNDING (p. 280).

Hopper and Thompson do not say specifically in this quoted section that the domain of grounding is for them the clause. A clause is either foregrounded or backgrounded in its entirety. The distinction made by Labov (1972) between narrative (foregrounded) and free (backgrounded) clauses is similar. The Athabaskan verse formally marks the last clause as the foregrounded clause.

In Athabaskan the clause often consists of nothing other than a verb. Where there are other elements in the clause or sentence they precede the verb in normal syntax. This emphasis on the last clause of the verse in grounding not only parallels the emphasis in the sentence on the verb in final position, it re-emphasizes this verb in foregrounding it. In this the verse further supports the position outlined by S. Scollon (1979) that Athabaskan tends to show a preference for process over object.

Some element other than a verb appears in the foregrounded position in a few cases. In these cases this final element is being emphasized even though it is not a full clause. These elements are most frequently noun phrases.

NARRATIVE STRUCTURE AS INTERACTION

Now that we have argued that the units of a narrative are formally marked as verse, stanza, and scene and that these units relate to emphasis, perspective, and memory, it remains to ask why a narrator should be concerned with such marking. The narrator, of course, knows the story he is to tell beforehand. We suggest that these concerns with narrative structure can only be understood if we see them being taken on behalf of the audience. The storyteller's goal is to create a story that will be highly intelligible to his audience without impinging on the audience's right to autonomy and noninterference. Scenes, stanzas, and verses are organized in a hierarchy of memory, perspective, and emphasis so that the audience will be guided in their interpretation of the story as an ongoing, real-time activity.

In our study of Chipewyan narrative (Scollon & Scollon 1979) we argued that the boundaries of narrative units could be seen as displaying the narrator's heightened attention to the perceptual needs of the audience at just those points. These markers, pauses, intonation shifts, changes in the pace of narration, changes in voice quality, changes of code or language or the increased use of gesture or postural cues all contribute to an increased interactive tension or involvement at just those points where the scene, stanza, or verse changes. That is, just where the pattern number, the perspective, or the emphasis is being marked, there is an increase in the mutual involvement of the storyteller and his audience.

As a narrator speaks, it is important for him to address his performance to his audience's perception of it. His audience must notice the correct succession of scenes, changes in perspective, and emphasis. The narrator must assume a great deal about his audience to do this. He must assume that the audience shares interpretive conventions for grammar and morphology, intonation, pausing, gesture, and body placement. These in turn signal higher level interpretation of time, location, events, and general human activity. In short, the audience must be able to understand the story.

The audience has the reciprocal responsibility of signalling its understanding to the narrator. The devices used range from lexicon to posture. Much of what is done consists of what Pawley and Syder (n.d.) have called "traffic signals." With these minimal gestures and comments the audience signals that the narration is proceeding well.

In addition, as we will discuss, the Athabaskan audience provides more elaborate confirmation in the form of completion and commentary on the narrative as it unfolds.

At first it appears that the role of the audience is to confirm the narrator's projected organization. It often happens, however, that this organization is not confirmed. The audience may fail to respond to a marked boundary or may respond where no boundary has been marked. When this happens the narrator may do one of two things. He may ignore the audience response and go on as if nothing had happened, or he may begin to do repair work. He may increase the marking, digress to expand his explanation or even incorporate the organization implied by the audience into his story. That is, he may accept the audience's responses as an equally valid conceptual organization.

We have documented a case of this latter situation in our Fort Chipewyan work. A man in telling us a story in Chipewyan told it in groups of twos and fours throughout. When he told the same story in English it was organized in groups of threes. At first we attributed the difference to a difference between the English and the Athabaskan storytelling traditions. As we looked more closely, however, it became clear than in the Chipewyan case we had been unable to respond because of our inability to understand Chipewyan at narrative speed. In the English version, though, we were able to respond and did, feeding to the narrator a set of organizational expectations around groups of threes with the mechanism of traffic signals. It was this set of audience expectations that the narrator skillfully incorporated into his performance and which were reflected in the narrative structure of the English version.

This same sensitivity to audience is reflected in all of the Athabaskan narratives to which we have had access. A particularly telling example is the life story of Chief Henry of Huslia (Jones 1980). Because of an error in the original tape recording a second recording of one section was made. The two recordings overlap in one section. It is interesting that the two recordings are virtually identical in stanza and scene structure. An important difference between the two versions is that one was recorded by a person who did not understand the story as it was being told in Koyukon. The other was recorded by a person who was able to interact meaningfully with Chief Henry during the narration.

Chief Henry tells in both versions of an event early in his life when he went to a store and bought a twenty-two rifle. In the version told to the non-understanding audience his interaction with the store-keeper is presented in a very matter-of-fact way. Something of the sort, "How much is the gun?" "Five dollars." In the version told to the person who understood, he reported that he had said something like, "I wonder if that gun over there might possibly be for sale?" and the storekeeper had said that it was.

The two versions are clearly distinguished in the politeness levels marked. Since we can presume that the original event could not have been carried on simultaneously in a multiplicity of styles we have to see this difference in politeness as relating to the audience of the story-telling. Chief Henry's shift in styles reflects attention to the audience, not the original storekeeper. The original words of the original event are secondary.

In summary then we suggest that the organization of Atha-baskan oral narrative is interactive. That is, we see it as unproductive to think of the narrative genre as an independent structural entity which is tailored to the oral performance. Rather, we see narrative structure as the result of a particular kind of interaction with an audience under particular kinds of conditions. Central to these conditions is the imposition of a view of reality while simultaneously main-taining a deep respect for the individuality of the audience.

Stanza as Action and Explanation

The stanza sometimes consists of several verses. We have said that the first of these introduces the point of view which is main-tained throughout the stanza. We have also said that in translation sets there was a near parallelism in stanzas and verses. Now we wish to look at one cause for the less than perfect parallelism.

In comparing two versions of a story we noticed in one place that the Athabaskan version and the English version had the same verses in the same stanza but in a different order. As we looked into it we found the difference to be of significance. In the Athabaskan ver-sion the narrator told of a man who had killed a Brush Indian (a quasi-human creature). He then told how he had buried him well. After this he said he felt very sorry about it because he had found out that the Brush Indian had been carrying a gift for him that he had mistaken as a knife. The sequence of the four verses is as follows:

a. kills (action)
b. buries (action)
c. regrets (evaluation)
d. realizes mistake (motive)

In the English version this same set of verses was told differently. The man killed the Brush Indian and then because he saw that he had mistaken the gift for a knife he felt sorry and had buried him carefully. In the English version the sequence of the four verses is as follows:

a. kills (action)
b. realizes mistake (motive)
c. regrets (evaluation)
d. buries (action)

We would argue that this difference is not accidental in either case but in fact represents the narrator's understanding of the different expectations of his audience. The Athabaskan order may be roughly glossed as *action* followed by explanation (that is, motivation, evaluation, clarification, and so on). The English order places the *explanation* in the first position to be followed by *action*.

A recurrent source of a parallel observation comes out in making translations. In preparing translations of Athabaskan texts it is frequently frustrating from the point of view of English that the explanation and motivation follows the description of the actions in stanzas. In working at translations with bilingual Athabaskan specialists it has frequently happened that we will translate a verse narrating some action. Then the non-Athabaskan will say something like, "Why did he do that?" The answer is always the same, "Wait. That's what comes next!"

This ordering in Athabaskan is, we believe, a product of the interaction of the representation of perspective and the non-intervening aspect of the bush consciousness. A stanza is begun with a verse in which an action (or the central perspective in non-action stanzas) is narrated. The stanza is then extended either until the narrator believes the audience has enough explanation to understand or, more importantly, the audience indicates its understanding through "traffic signals" or some other response.

The English ordering of explanation followed by action is consonant with the decontextualization and noninteractiveness of the modern consciousness. Actions are explained, evaluated, and motivated by the text in advance of their description. Actions follow as the logical implications of pre-existing values or ideas. It is in fact highly consistent with rule by law that in the English ordering the action follows its prior definition.

The narrator does not presume to tell his audience how to think or interpret actions in the Athabaskan stanza. Actions are presented directly and as much as possible without interpretation. Further explanation and motivation are added where called for by the audience.

The Athabaskan Stanza as a Model of Interaction

We now can see that the Athabaskan stanza is a case of a linguistic form, a discourse form, mirroring the interactive patterns of the society. Of course, it is our point that this is more than a mirroring. It is an identity. The stanza in narrative is a result of non-intervention in interaction, just as is Athabaskan taciturnity with strangers in interethnic communication. We said in chapter two that often Athabaskans prefer to observe a person's actions before engaging in talk while English speakers prefer to use talk as a way of regulating a person's actions. This we claim is another instance of the same phenomenon.

The parallels run throughout Athabaskan communicative activity and in interethnic communication. For example, Athabaskans often find the attitude of non-Athabaskans offensive when the latter order native crafts. It is sometimes complained that the person making the order expects it to be made to particular measurements, with particular designs, and with particular materials. This insistence on the tailoring of a parka, for example, is found abusive by native craftswomen and an infringement of their right as artists to design and complete the garment they choose. The appropriate attitude they suggest is to have the parka made as the craftswoman sees fit and then if adjustments need to be made to do those oneself.

Hippler and Conn (1972) have said that traditional Athabaskan legal process was very similar. There was no concept of an illegal act as such. An act was regarded as bad or dangerous to the extent that it disrupted an individual's or a group's activities. There was no fixed punishment as such, but rather some reparation was decided on by the elders. Something had to be done to restore the offended individual's autonomy. The seriousness of a "crime" was judged by the extent of the disruption. It was not evaluated in and of itself.

This judgment after the fact is of course consistent with the Athabaskan action/explanation ordering and at variance with the legal system of the modern consciousness. In that system all acts are defined in advance by means of the legal code and penalties prescribed for violation. The seriousness of the offence is judged in relation to an *a priori* scheme of justification, not in relation to any actual personal or social result.

It is not difficult to see then all contracts and even treaties as examples of the explanation/action ordering of the modern consciousness. A contract such as the legal code defines action of all involved parties on *a priori* grounds. Later adjustments can only be interpreted in terms of the original contract, treaty, and definitions.

The action/explanation ordering of the bush consciousness is of course consistent with the prohibition of speaking of the future. The concept of *injíh* or the taboo on anticipating the future is realized in letting any motivation or evaluation follow the action that is undertaken as subsequent circumstances dictate.

The ordering of the stanza is a reflection in discourse of the reality set by means of patterns of interaction. The English or modern consciousness ordering of explantion and action implies a closing of the system around formal, *a priori* definitions on the one hand, and on the other a decontextualization from the contexts of situational and interactive relevance. The Athabaskan or bush consciousnesses ordering of action and explanation implies an open system, a situationally interactive system in which one person is careful not to interfere with the autonomy of other individuals.

The Athabaskan Verse as a Riddle

Athabaskans often complain of elicited and dictated stories that they are not very realistic. On further questioning it usually is said that what is missing is the speech of the audience. When people go on they say that the audience must at least say something like *ehe* after "everything the storyteller says" and will even go so far as to say that sometimes the audience will finish things for the narrator. Lacking a fuller understanding of what counts as "everything the storyteller says" we were unable at first to be very specific about when and how the audience responds. The verse was the analytical concept needed. The audience is expected to respond at the end of each verse.

When we got more specific about what sorts of responses were expected it became clear that the best reponse is to finish what the narrator is saying. Recalling now that the function of the verse is grounding and that the foregrounded material comes last what this means is that the skillful audience is expected to say the foregrounded clauses. If we identify the foregrounded clauses with the real heart of the story this means that the audience is supposed to tell the story. The role of the narrator in this reversal of positions is to provide just enough backgrounded information so that the audience will be able to guess the verse's conclusion and say it in his own words.

We have known through an early study of Jette (1913) and more recent work by Dauenhauer (1976b, 1977) that riddles were important for Athabaskans. Recently we began to suspect that there was a more direct connection of riddles with narrative. When people describe a function for riddles in Athabaskan it is often said that they are to prepare people for the "high language." They see riddles as schooling in guessing meanings, in reading between the lines, in anticipating outcomes and in indirectness. In short, riddles provide a schooling in non-intervention. They are not so much a test of knowledge and language ability, although they are certainly that, as they are practice in isolating what we call themes or metonyms in the next chapter. A skillful riddler will tease a listener all around a point with a sequence of riddles until the riddler breaks through to the obvious and voices it. It is this breaking through to the central point that is trained with the riddle. A skillful listener will guess the riddle quickly no matter how indirect or circuitous the riddler may become.

We see the verse then as a type of riddle and the narrative as an extended sequence of riddles. The best telling of a story is the briefest. It depends on a close understanding between the narrator and the audience. At the slightest mention of a narrative theme the audience will respond with a completion. The stanza does not need to be expanded with explanations or motivations. These are understood. When all themes have been suggested the story is completed. In this view even the title of some traditional narratives can be seen as tellings in the form of riddles. For example, the well known Chipewyan story "His Grandmother Raised Him" has the form of a riddle, the answer to which are the themes of the story—a small boy found, raised, turned caribou, and so forth.

At the other extreme stories may become extremely lengthy or inconclusive where the understanding of the audience is low. As the narrator begins, the verse brings no response. The stanza must be expanded. These expansions tend to dilute the narrative impact and still elicit no relevant response. Other themes are tried and finally the enterprise is given up—sometimes in mid-narrative. Narrators faced with an unresponding audience normally chose either briefly to summarize, to leave the situation, or in some exceptional cases to fictionalize an understanding audience. This final group of narrators includes those who have made some commitment to the development of the modern consciousness.

NARRATIVE AND THE SOCIAL CONSTRUCTION OF REALITY

The highly interactive, nonintervening Athabaskan oral narrative performance is the way it is because of what is being done. Where folklorists and others have conceived of oral narrative as the literal passing on of a text, the Athabaskan oral performance and others like it have been difficult to understand. It has appeared that texts were not well known, that traditions were highly eroded and that elders and tradition bearers did not hold the high respect of other members of the society. We prefer to view the narrative context as not one of passing on tradition, although it is that as well, nor simply one of entertainment, although it is also that. We see Athabaskan storytelling as the social construction of reality. It is the imposition of a view of the world under conditions where the highest respect must be paid to the view of the world held by the audience. By expanding the stanza only to the extent necessary and by allowing the audience the opportunity in the verse to phrase the core of the story in his own words, the narrator pays the respect due to his listener's right to autonomy and independence.

As we have said above in discussing the nonintervening aspect of the bush consciousness, the ideal learning situation for a child or a young person is to be able to hear the stories of elders. The ideal situation described is that of elders speaking to each other as narrator and audience with the child in a third, observational role. In this situation, the child learns from both the narrator and the audience. From the narrator the child learns the strategies of nonintervention in the presentation of his ideas. From the audience the child learns how one becomes a sensitive, alert, and synthesizing observer. By the same token, because the child is not directly required to respond to the narratives, his own autonomy is respected at a time in his life when it is likely to be highly vulnerable. While this three-party narrative situation may not always obtain, those who are able to learn in this way are regarded as very fortunate and all value contexts in which they can hear the narrative interaction of elders.

CHIEF HENRY OF HUSLIA'S LIFE STORY

Now we will look at a short excerpt from the life story of Chief Henry (Jones, 1979) that we referred to previously. This section has been chosen to exemplify the line, verse, and stanza structure of one story which is quite typical. In the presentational format used a line is represented by a line of type. That is, there is a pause at the end of each line. A double space represents the end of a verse and a triple space represents stanza breaks.

At the time of the story Chief Henry was a young man of about fifteen years of age. He had been hunting with his family's group when he had decided to go look for his uncle's group. After a long day of travel he had arrived at their camp hungry and exhausted. They had not seen each other in a long time.

In the first verse he is told to eat and the others do not speak to him while he eats and regains his strength. Notice two things here. First, he is not expected to speak and clarify his comings and goings before a long period of quiet has passed. Second, the others go on speaking as if he were not present. That is, it is not silence as such that is practiced but nonintervention or noninteraction. They do not speak to him because that would require him to respond. In this is reflected an assumption that speech requires interaction and that respect requires noninteraction.

In the second stanza Chief Henry's uncle is said to be the spokesman for the group. Notice he is not speaking here to outsiders but directing the group itself. That is, the term "spokesman" is used rather than "leader," "chief," "boss," or some other such managerial term. His direction is phrased as his own wishes. It is something he wants which the rest of the group may take or leave. This wish of

Ts'ʉhʉ ts'a
kk'ʉdaa
        —Tłaa tłaa k'eehonh—
sahadnee. Dahoon koon dosahaadaatłlik.

Dahoon kkanaahadilghus.

Ts'ʉh kk'ʉdaa
k'aaghason' ts'ʉh
        —Ts'ʉh dodot
        dodot hʉts'ihn ło go dint'aanh?—
kk'ʉdaa koon siłnee go ada sil'aa k'aal hanaayee.

        —Oho'-
beesnee.

Ts'ʉhʉ
kk'ʉdaa hataalyo'.

        —Tłeegho neełyił nokkanaazitolghus dahʉgh eesee
        do'o da go
        sidnaa'
        biditseega hoolaan ghasghonh yiłneey ghʉ ees
        tłaa neełghʉ sodidił da
        neełyił nokkanaahaditolghus ts'a hʉkk'aat—
nee.
Yoogh don hʉt'aan tł'eegho hał
neełyił kkanaahadilghus ts'a hʉkk'aa dahagheet'aa'.

Ts'ʉh
        —Go kk'ʉdaa ts'a gheel go koon sidnaa'
        bidziyh nilaan yos dinaa oho niłiynaatłtseen gheel go
        koon biyah k'ahozilniy hee—
nee.

So
then
    —Wait and eat—
they told me and refrained from speaking to me while I ate.*

And meanwhile they talked to each other.

And so
I ate and then
    From down here
    did you come from down here?—
My dear old uncle asked me, being the spokesman for the group.

    —Yes-
I told him.

So then
he started talking.

    So that we can all talk to each other
    I would like for us
    to meet at the place
    over there where
    my child said
    he caught two calves—**
he said.

A long time ago
people used to really like to talk to each other.

So then
    —Now that we're finished hunting
    —we're struggling*** back home with a little caribou
        meat our son has gathered for us—
he said.

*They refrained from talking to him while he was eating because they knew he was tired from a long walk, and hungry. Out of consideration for him they carried on their normal conversation as if he weren't there while he finished eating and regained his strength.

**The two calves he is referring to are the cow and calf that his son-in-law Moses Henry caught the day before. He diminished them out of respect.

***Rather than saying that they had plenty of meat then, in fact all that they could pull, he said that they had enough. He is trying to avoid sounding as if he is bragging. In our way it is important not to sound as if you are bragging when you are talking about accomplishments.

Eeyit
huyiɫ go sil'aa
Solfok
William haydagheenee' hun
　　—Oho'
　　aditugh ant'aay dideenee—
nee.

Ts'uh yoogh
go ahadinh haɫ kk'udaa
tsaay yiɫ
dakk'un yiɫ
k'idotɫaa' yiɫ
kk'udaa k'aadeenh.

Go hunh zo tsaay
zo
ts'it'aanh
baaba ts'eeɫt'aan dahoonh.

K'idotɫaa' yiɫ dakkun yiɫ k'ahat'aanh.

Go yoogh
dinaa een
sooga dinaaghu neehadagheeɫkiyhdla aahaa haboho k'its'oogheekkaat.

Ts'uh kk'odahun'
kk'udaa koon
yoo'oots'a no'eediyo.

　　—Sidnaa
　　nagganaa' y̦aan' yoodo' notodolee?—
yiɫnee.

　　—Aa
　　ts'aa(1) yoodot
　　eetaa' habugh tɫiditaaghsliɫ dahugh biyiɫ notaaghsdoɫ—
yiɫnee.

And then
my late uncle
who used to be called
South Fork William
      —Yes,
      what you say is right,—
he said.

And by then
their group
was out of
tea
tobacco
and shells.

But our group
at least
had tea
even though we didn't have food.

They also had shells and tobacco.

Different people in our group
had given us marten skins with which
we had bought things for them.

So the next morning
he came back over
again.
      —My child,
      is your friend going back (to the other group) by himself?—
he asked him.

      —Oh,
      it's O.K. (I'll go) down there with him
      so that I can spend a night with my parents.—
he told him.

his is then answered by the other uncle called South Fork William. This is the formal response required by the spokesman's statement. Notice, again, that speech is seen as requiring interaction. A spokesman must be answered by another spokesman. Each speaks as if for himself but implicitly for the group. In these formal exchanges about group plans the same reserve and respect for the autonomy of others are reflected.

Linguistically we can also observe the free verb stem *nee* ("Ø said" and by implication "he said"). In non-formal speech some person-marking prefix is normally required. Here, however, the speech is marked only as "said," not as directed to any participant or from any participant. Morphologically then we see a reflection of the indirectness and nonintervention required by a situation of directing others' plans.

In a less formal setting the same uncle tells his child to accompany Chief Henry back to his group. Here the directive is phrased in the form of the question, "Is your friend going back by himself?" Where the power disparity is much greater the linguistic means are somewhat more direct but remain nevertheless very respectful of the right to nonintervention of the boy.

Finally, we can observe in Chief Henry's uncle's statement that his son had caught two calves the same playing down of one's own accomplishments or the accomplishments of one's group. In fact, they had plentiful food and were grateful for it but it was phrased as having little and just struggling along.

This example has brought us to the edge of what can be done in an expository format. Further understanding of the bush consciousness and its means of expression in discourse requires discourse means more in keeping with that reality set. One needs to hear stories to go much further.

ABSTRACTING THEMES IN NARRATIVE INTERACTION

We see the bush consciousness as organizing knowledge through the use of themes. This form of organization is highly metonymic. The world is known as situations, processes and events which are characterized parsimoniously with the briefest of references to whole situations. It is possible in this way to integrate a wide range of personal experience into the experience of tradition while retaining a feeling of individual control of knowledge and understanding.

Stories consist of a set of themes and a pattern of interaction. In the presentation of the story the narrator is sensitive to the need for autonomy and integration of knowledge of the audience. In the best telling little more than the themes are suggested and the audience is able to interpret those themes as highly contextualized in his own experience.

We have been at pains to suggest the extent to which the bush consciousness and its patterns of discourse differ from the modern consciousness and essayist literacy. It is important to point out that the interactive Athabaskan narrative at least resembles some of the best in western poetic and narrative traditions. Chatman (1978) speaks of Hemingway's careful avoidance of evaluation and description of the inner states of his characters in terms that are much like ours in speaking of the Athabaskan stanza. Hemingway's careful avoidance of any suggestion about how the reader should interpret events is much like the Athabaskan avoidance of telling the audience too much, of violation of the integrity of the audience through too much intervention.

In a recent interview Ekbert Faas (1978) asked the poet Gary Snyder how he knew where to end a poem. Snyder's answer was much like our description of the Athabaskan verse. Snyder said that he takes a poem up to the point where the reader can take it over for himself. This reticence, this attitude of not telling the reader but rather leading the reader to undertake his own work of understanding is characteristic of the best in human communication.

While we have characterized the modern consciousness and essayist literacy as one pole and the bush consciousness and thematic abstraction as the other pole of an opposition in communicative values, we now wish to suggest that this opposition does not successfully characterize all individuals as either Athabaskan (or Indian) or English (or White). There are individuals who are successful in managing both reality sets to some extent, and there are certainly situations in the modern world calling for the appropriate use of one or the other of these communicative systems. What is at issue in our work is how confusion or conflict among these communicative systems is managed and with what gains and what losses.

Six

Abstracting Themes:
A Chipewyan Two-Year-Old

THE ABSTRACTION OF THEMES

We have only recently come to realize the degree to which Western or modern consciousness has been affected by widespread literacy. Since the Enlightenment in Europe, literacy has been highly valued as the hallmark of intelligence. It has assumed central importance as both the means of education and the ultimate goal of the schooling process (Olson 1977b). From a historical perspective, Goody (1977) traces the development of literacy as the decontextualization of language from the domain of speaking and its transformation into a unimodal visual display.

The pervasiveness of the literate orientation in Western society has obscured for us the fact that literacy is the result of early and continual learning, not something that develops in the natural course of maturation. Teachers of young children use a style of speaking that Cook-Gumperz (1978) has suggested is instrumental in developing the literate orientation. By teaching children to pay attention to exact wording more than to contextualization cues in following instructions this interactive style of teachers works toward developing skills in decontextualization which are necessary for literacy.

We have suggested in chapter three that the decontextualization of the literate orientation consists of two central aspects. The first of these involves a shift in the information structure toward a higher degree of explicitness. In written text there is a higher percentage of new information to given information (Cook-Gumperz & Gumperz 1978). Logical relations are explicitly formulated lexically and syntactically in written text but prosodically in spoken English text. Indexical use of the context is limited as the text itself becomes its own context.

The second sort of decontextualization is that involved in the fictionalization of the audience (Ong 1977) and the author (Foucault 1977). In writing, the author creates an audience, a public to which the text is addressed. To the extent that this audience is unknown to the author at the time of writing it is a fiction created in writing. As texts speak to generation after generation of readers the audience recreates itself quite independently of the author's original work. The author becomes fictionalized by the same token. As the unknown readership relates to the author through the text, the author is created or fictionalized by the audience. As an active fiction necessary for the distance required by the decontextualization of the information structure, the author works toward self-effacement in relation to the text.

We have argued in chapter four that by the third birthday a child in the Western tradition may be well on the way toward developing the decontextualization necessary for literacy. By developing the prosodic structures associated with oral reading a child makes important steps toward integrating the information structure characteristic of written text. At the same time the child's ability to use third person references in relation to the self indicates a degree of fictionalization of the self necessary for both authorship and readership.

Our concern in this chapter is not with literacy but with what might for the moment be called "orality." It is an indication of how central literacy is to our thinking that we have practically a terminological vacuum for referring to any other orientation. The terms that are available tend to be negative, "nonliterate," or worse "illiterate," misleading, "tribal," romantic, "natural," or to smack of infantilism, "oral," or savagery, "primitive." These terms neither do justice to the phenomenon we wish to look at in societies that are primarily not literate nor do they represent nonliterate aspects of our own society. In this chapter we will refer to the intellectual quality under consideration as "thematic abstraction." It is the quality that characterizes the narrative interactions discussed in chapter five.

There have been various suggestions in the literature that a quality something like "thematic abstraction" is present wherever from our point of view prodigious feats of memory are in evidence. These are especially the production of long narratives in what are usually called oral traditions. Goody (n.d.) has argued that the reproductions of the Bagre myth for the Lo Dagaa in Northern Ghana were not cases of exact line-by-line memory as he had once believed but rather reconstructions around a sequential structure of themes and events. These thematic structures are neither as close to the surface as word-by-word recall nor as deep and hypothetical as some mythologists' analytical structures. We would like to call the cognitive orientation underlying this sort of memory "thematic abstraction."

In other traditions as well this quality of thematic abstraction has been suggested as being the foundation on which traditional genres are remembered and performed. Tedlock (1975) has for some time argued against the assumption of an 'Urtext" or an invariable form of the oral text in folklore studies. It is his view that the text that is performed is the result of an interaction between some structural conception of the story and an important integration of the ongoing situation of the performance. Foster (1974) in his study of the Iroquois Longhouse tradition, also has suggested the importance of understanding the themes around which a performer builds his performance as central, not any literal memorization of a traditional text.

We would like to argue that this ability which we recognize in the performance of epics, folk narratives, and Longhouse speeches reflects a general orientation to both language and knowledge that is a highly developed, well integrated aspect of intelligence, not simply the residue of the absence of literacy. While this is not difficult to appreciate when we are confronted with an oral performance of a myth that takes several days to perform and is many thousands of lines in length, it is somewhat more difficult to appreciate for the literate person in the seemingly cryptic single statement in a public meeting by an important American Indian leader. Looking further into the formally elegant, linguistically parsimonious, but immature narratives of a ten year old Athabaskan child, it takes a great work of understanding to see that in these narratives is reflected the same quality of thematic abstraction that we value in the poet or in the narrative exchanges of experienced elders.

THE ROLE OF CULTURE-SPECIFIC THEMES IN RECALL AND COMPREHENSION

We mentioned in the last chapter that recently psychologists and others working in memory have pointed to the importance of culture-specific schemata in recall and comprehension of stories (Kintsch 1977, Kintsch & Greene 1978). In Kintsch's work it was observed that subjects who came from a European-based tradition were able to remember with a higher degree of accuracy the structures of stories selected from the repertoire of Europe's folklore. Where stories came from the Athabaskan tradition the same subjects did worse at recall and comprehension tasks. The basic problem was related to the organization of European folktales in episodic structures of three parts which agreed with the expectations of the subjects. The Athabaskan stories which were organized around episodic structures of four parts suffered the loss of one of the parts or merger of two of the four parts.

This work points to the general importance of organizational schemata which are not universal attributes of human cognition but rather specifically learned as part of one's cultural training. We have also described a case in which a story told in Chipewyan was organized about episodic structures of two and four parts but when the same story was told in English it was organized about episodic structures of three parts. The difference in this case in organization was attributed to the interaction of the narrator with the audience. In the English version his audience responded throughout in such a way that the narrator introduced new segmenting formulas and created what was really a jointly produced narrative structure. It is clear in this case that both narrator and audience have approached the story performance with a set of expectations about the thematic structure of the narrative that reflect different cultural traditions.

Now we would like to argue that not only are there culture-specific organizational or interpretative schemata that organize our thinking about narrative events, but that in some contexts there is an absolutely higher value placed on such schematic organization. In our comparisons of the stories of a "literate" child with those of a nonliterate child in chapter four, we found that even though the "literate" child at two years of age could not yet read or write, her stories showed the properties of decontextualization that form the foundational orientation to literacy. The other child, who at ten years of age could both read and write as well as type, nevertheless organized her narratives by thematically abstracting out the four-part episodic structure and preserving this through both oral and written versions. Her written version was a formally condensed, succinct statement of the essential themes of her more diffuse and wordy spoken version. Neither version, however, showed significant decontextualization either in the information structure or in the fictionalization of the self as author or as character.

Because we have now seen this highly parsimonious abstraction of the thematic structure done successfully by children in as wide a geographic range as from Fort Chipewyan on Lake Athabasca in northern Alberta to villages on the Upper Kuskokwim in western Alaska, we believe it to be characteristic of at least northern Athabaskans. Of course, it should not be surprising that the quality of thematic abstraction so fundamental to the oral narrative tradition should be learned early in life. We will in this chapter argue that thematic abstraction is the result of a lifelong learning process that is characterized in general by nonintervention. We will look closely at the evidence we have for this ability in the third year of life. We will describe in some detail the orientation of one Chipewyan two year old child. By looking at his interactions with his caregivers we will suggest the mechanisms by which a child is socialized to the abstraction of themes and the bush consciousness.

A Mother's Decision

The child we will be describing in this study is the youngest of about half a dozen siblings. By two he was speaking Chipewyan to some extent and acknowledged to be doing so by other members of the speech community. Because this is unusual in the community of Fort Chipewyan we will need to digress to give the reader some of the background of both this child and the community.

THE COMMUNITY OF FORT CHIPEWYAN

For the past 200 years Fort Chipewyan, Alberta, has been a center of trapping and exploration for the whole Northwest. It was from Fort Chipewyan that Roderick Mackenzie set out on his explorations leading both to the Arctic Ocean and the Pacific Ocean. There are now four languages used in the community because in this long history many interests have focused on Fort Chipewyan: English, French, Chipewyan, and Cree (Scollon & Scollon 1979). These four languages are not equally distributed throughout the community. Since the 1950s English has been most widely used in the community. This is closely related to the transfer of the school from church control to control by Indian Affairs. Before that French was the privileged language of education and religion. French is still closely related to religious matters but beyond the church there is little French spoken.

The two native languages, Chipewyan and Cree, have been used in the Fort Chipewyan area from before white settlement 200 years ago. Just where and when the two groups were in the Lake Athabaska area is not clear but they are now both well established there. There is a difference between these two languages, however, in the relative positions of prestige they hold. Cree is identified by most people as the "high" native language and it is asserted that there is no "high" Chipewyan language.

As a result of the different functional distributions of languages at Fort Chipewyan, speakers of Chipewyan are often quite reserved about displaying the ability to speak Chipewyan in public. One much more often hears Cree, but even that is reserved to some extent.

The Bilingual Dilemma

Chipewyan speakers at Fort Chipewyan have various ideas about the learning and use of language that independently relate to fairly well observed cultural expectations about language for Athabaskans. The first of these is that children do not begin to speak until they are about five years of age or so. They are not expected to speak well until considerably older and really careful, sensitive use of the grammatical system is not expected of anyone but older people. It is assumed that Athabaskan languages take a lifetime to learn well. This expectation is often stated in so many words and we have corroborated it with many observations both at Fort Chipewyan and in Alaska. As a converse statement of this expectation people often register surprise that people who speak English and Chinese expect their children to carry on conversations when they are only two or three years old. This is often regarded as exotic behavior and on the whole inexplicable.

The ability to learn language is not tied to any overt production of speech for Athabaskans. The fact that one does not speak does not necessarily imply anything about one's ability to speak. This may be related to the different linkage of dominance and display for Athabaskans (see chapter two). Where the child is thought of as being in the subordinate position and where subordination is linked to spectatorship there is no reason why the child should display his ability to speak for adults. Adults should display their abilities for the child to learn. As we have said, for Athabaskans keeping one's silence is an appropriate way to indicate that one is taking a subordinate, respectful role in the interaction with another person. It is not interpreted as ignorance. In many conversations with Athabaskans we observed that where the listener remained silent it was usually interpreted as understanding and showing respect, not as a failure to understand. In the same way children who do not begin to speak until five years of age or older are interpreted as growing up respectfully, not as being "language-delayed." A high value is placed on good listening, as we have said above in our discussion of narrative interactions.

A second expectation about language use held by Athabaskans at Fort Chipewyan is that one does not speak in front of someone in a language they cannot understand. Generally in situations where there are several participants a language is chosen which allows all participants to speak and understand. Where this is not possible it is common to apologize for speaking in front of someone. A graphic example of this expectation may be drawn from two softball games that took place in another Athabaskan community, Arctic Village, Alaska. One evening we watched at a distance while a group of people played softball. All of the talk during the game by players and spectators alike was in Kutchin. The next evening one of us was asked to play. All of the talk during the second game, again by both players and spectators, was in English. The only factor that had changed was the language of one of the participants. In the second case one of the participants could not speak or understand Kutchin. that was sufficient reason for some dozen people to speak in a different language.

We have observed this same expectation at the extreme western end of the northern Athabaskan area, in Holy Cross,

Alaska. We feel that the expectation that one will not speak in front of people in a language they cannot understand is a significant aspect of Athabaskan linguistic etiquette, again showing respect for the potential audience.

A third idea people at Fort Chipewyan have about language is that it is easier to speak and understand Cree or English than Chipewyan. In this respect there was agreement with people at Arctic Village who also expressed the idea that English was easier for children to learn than Kutchin. We realize that this may in fact be an indirect way of saying that people feel it is preferable for some reason for children not to learn Athabaskan, perhaps because of social pressures against its use. We feel, though, that it is probably simply true in some sense. The Athabaskan consonant system is much more complex than that of either English or Cree. This shows up directly in later mastery of the full adult consonant system. At the same time, the morphological complexity of the Athabaskan verb is formidable by comparison with English, though not so much by comparison with Cree. We expect from our own experience that one arrives much sooner at the point where one can say things intelligibly in any of the languages at Fort Chipewyan than in Chipewyan.

These three expectations about language learning and language use have a structural result that in the bilingual situation leads to lesser and lesser learning of Chipewyan. Although people do speak to very young infants in Chipewyan, there is a tendency later on to use English. One preadolescent child spoke to our one week old baby in Chipewyan. It was the only Chipewyan we ever heard this child use. In other contexts she adamantly refused to admit she could speak or understand even when speaking with her grandparents. This may indicate a feeling that Chipewyan is appropriate for speaking to babies.

The baby often begins to speak within a year or so, however. This speech is usually understood as being in English or Cree. At least one of these languages is present in the environments of most children at Fort Chipewyan. Because of the belief that these languages are easier to speak than Chipewyan, and because children are not expected to speak Chipewyan until five years of age or so, people interpret the early speech of the child as being in one of these languages. As speech develops in Cree or English the second expectation begins to come into effect. People say that they feel they should speak to the baby in English or Cree because that is what the baby understands. Although we have said that the baby's not speaking Chipewyan is not in itself evidence that he or she cannot understand Chipewyan, if all the evidence is that the child speaks English people feel that is the language they should speak in return.

The structural result of this situation is that the critical environment that the child needs to learn Chipewyan is removed. The child no longer is spoken to in Chipewyan. Now the only opportunities to hear Chipewyan are all in contexts where there are monolingual Chipewyan speakers present. In the modern speech community these people are becoming quite rare, so before the child has a chance to hear enough Chipewyan spoken to him and to learn enough to be able to say a few things, the situation becomes altered into one in which English or Cree is assumed to be the child's language.

We have suggested above that it is probably true to say that in a primary sense Chipewyan is more difficult to learn than English or Cree. It is certainly true in the sense that one needs a broader command of the language as a whole before one can say even fairly simple things because of the complex integration of so much of the basic information about actors, propositions, mood, and aspect within the verb. This is not something that can be changed without fundamentally changing the nature of the Athabaskan language.

It is difficult because of this to suggest that people ought to expect children to speak Athabaskan earlier in life. In fact, the only dimension that it seems possible to do anything about from the standpoint of the individual is the attitude toward speaking to people and especially children in a language they do not understand. In the case study we will be looking at this is just where the mother of this family was able to have an important effect on her children's language.

A CHIPEWYAN FAMILY

In the case we will be looking at here, the family had moved into Fort Chipewyan during the year we were there. The father of this family had been raised in the school at Fort Chipewyan and as a result spoke very little Chipewyan. There is some disagreement about this statement that should be clarified. His children asserted that he could and did speak Chipewyan. His wife, however, said that he spoke very little. We feel that the children who were then under pressure at Fort Chipewyan to deny their own ability to use the language were seeking to maintain a strong self-image as a Chipewyan family and to do this felt they needed to say their father did speak Chipewyan. At any rate, he had for some years been chief of a small group of Chipewyans to the south of Fort Chipewyan.

The mother of this family (CM) had come from a town in Saskatchewan where people are said to speak Chipewyan. She was raised by older people who insisted on her using the language and using it well. She was one of the fortunate individuals mentioned above who had her elders "in her ears," who had had the benefit of listening in on elders' conversation. There is no doubt of her ability with the language.

As she began to raise children she fell into the pattern that we have described. She spoke at first to them in Chipewyan but as they began to use English she had shifted into using English with them. As she told us, she had assumed that when the time came they would be able to start to speak Chipewyan. As that time came and passed without any evidence of the children being able to use the language, she made a unilaterial decision to refuse to speak to the children in English. She had to do this in the face of the expectation that one would not speak to someone in a language he did not understand. She was afraid, however, that her children would grow up unable to speak Chipewyan if she did not do something about it herself. As the mother and primary caregiver of these children she saw herself as the one responsible if they did not learn Chipewyan.

The result of CM's decision is striking. All of her younger children now speak Chipewyan. One can date CM's decision by the Chipewyan abilities of the children. The ones above a certain age do speak Chipewyan but not as well as the younger ones. All of them speak English.

We are interested in this case study for two reasons. The first reason is that we have seen that so-called "language loss" is not inevitable nor is it even irreversible. By making a unilateral decision that was not easy by any means, this mother was able to significantly affect the language abilities of four or five individuals. These children are among the most self-assertive speakers of an Athabaskan language that we have seen. They are proud of their ability to speak Chipewyan and understand it for the important knowledge that it is.

Our second reason for being interested in this case is that this family is consciously and actively seeking to bring up their children within a tradition that is different from the literate orientation of the school. They see this tradition as part of their identity and highly value it. They do not see it as the residue of the absence of literacy. We feel that the material we discuss is evidence for the early stages of socialization to an integrated tradition, the bush consciousness.

The child we will be looking at in this case we will call CB for "Chipewyan boy." He was the youngest child in the family at the time of our study. He was two years old. His two older sisters took care of him during most of the time they were not in school. Although there are some minor differences between the two older sisters, in this material we are not making any distinction between them. We will refer to either one of them as COS for "Chipewyan older sister." They were our neighbors and our own two year old daughter Rachel played with CB and the two COS's during much of the time the older girls were not in school.

We will make little reference in the discussion that follows to contexts outside of our home or to situations in which interaction was with adults or with anyone other than COS. This is for three reasons. The first is that this situation has provided us with our best material and most solid documentation. Tape recording which is at all times difficult in Fort Chipewyan is even more difficult in the presence of young children in the context of their own homes. Documentation came easier in our home where it could be contextualized as an ordinary activity and we prefer to exemplify this case with our best documentation.

The second reason we have not referred to other contexts relates to the general view Athabaskans take of paying close attention to young children. Because close attention to young children threatens a high level of intervention in their affairs it is regarded as quite dangerous. It has in fact for Athabaskans the potential of child abuse and is carefully avoided. Our observations of children had to be conducted in a very circumspect manner being careful not to subject the children involved to any amount of intervention in their affairs. Consequently, documentation was problematical and largely restricted to notes written after the event. Our observations of other children at Fort Chipewyan and in a number of villages in Alaska have largely served as checks of hypotheses generated by our primary data, the data partially presented here.

The third reason then is that it seems most effective to present the material collected in half a dozen or more villages and with many children as a single clear case which we have observed repeated from Lake Athabasca to the Lower Yukon River area.

THEMES AND METONYMS

We can think of abstracting themes as being a matter of "chunking." The substance of knowledge is chunked in such a way that highly complex activities or behaviors or situations are seen as wholes, as units within some broader conceptualization. As a way of trying to be more specific about this admittedly vague approach to thematic abstraction, we will look at two types of chunking that were so salient in our early observations that we kept fairly complete notes even though at the time we did not see just why they were of importance. We can gloss these two types of chunking as role expectations and as situational chunking.

Role Expectations as Heightened Contextualization

One evening S. Scollon was working with COS on telling and transcribing stories. In order to overhear them, R. Scollon left the bedroom that was used as a study and made popcorn in the kitchen where the others were working. A bit later R. Scollon began sweeping up the popcorn that had fallen on the floor. COS became upset, took away the broom and finished the job. As R. Scollon returned from the bathroom a few minutes later CB stood at the door of the study and looking very sternly at R. Scollon motioned for him to sit down at his chair in front of the desk.

On another occasion some days later CB "caught" R. Scollon folding laundry in the bedroom. He pulled the clothes out of his hands, took his hand and led him up the hallway to the study. There he again pointed to the chair and said, "Here. Here."

A few days later R. Scollon was playing with Rachel, our daughter. CB took Rachel by the hand and said, " kú˙ kú˙ come," (Come!" or "now come!") and led her away as he motioned R.

Scollon at the door of the study to go in to his seat. To R. Scollon he said, "Daddy wé" ("Daddy over there!").

It is clear from examples like these that CB as well as COS had very definite conceptions of appropriate behavior for individuals in particular contexts. It was R. Scollon's role while at home to sit at a desk and work. It was COS's role to clean up. It was Rachel's and CB's role to play. Violations of these role expectations were always met with corrections. If the violation was not corrected the children left the house. It was apparently intolerable to watch people step out of these role expectations.

We began to make notes about cases such as these because they struck us as being much more strongly stereotyped than anything we had seen with our own daughter or in children we had observed elsewhere. Far from being passive expectations it sometimes seemed as if CB was trying to help us learn these expectations. One day CB started looking around among the toys scattered here and there. He found Rachel's toy wrench. He took it and tried to hand it to the two month old infant Tommy. He then found Rachel's spoon and gave it to S. Scollon. Finally he found a pen and gave it to R. Scollon. In this case he was not motivated by an obsession with cleaning up the house. That never bothered him. Nor was he concerned with relocating us in our respective tasks. In the earlier examples he had shown that he could very effectively get R. Scollon to go back to his seat at the desk. In this case we feel he was using these objects and their distribution to refer to the roles of the respective individuals. With his distribution of symbols, which we would call metonyms, if they had been words, CB had said something like, "The baby is a boy and works with wrenches, the mother is a woman and cooks, the father is a writer and writes." We would argue that CB's interest in this case was with symbolizing in a succinct way the role expectations of the group of people present.

This set of role expectations develops early. On one occasion COS was holding our baby who was about one month old at the time. She held him so that he could only look toward his mother. As R. Scollon called his name he searched for his father. When he did get his father in his line of vision, COS put up her hand to obstruct his view. There was nothing that indicated that she was teasing or playing in doing this. She was simply doing what was necessary to direct the infant's attention toward the mother and to intercept communication between the infant and the father.

On another occasion when COS was baking with S. Scollon CB started to get up by the table where they were working. COS pushed him away and said, "Go do man's work." CB's learning of this message was quite clear in the occasion when he came into the house, saw R. Scollon washing dishes and ran out again. As we have said, these children found it difficult to stay in the same situation with people who were flaunting their violations of expected behavior.

What is striking in this case to us is the difference in orientation between our role expectations and those of the CF children. On this occasion when CB ran out of the house he was wearing red barrettes. He had shoulder length hair and by our standards looked very much like a little girl. We found that our expectations were very much oriented to the visual whereas the orientation we are describing here is oriented to the behavioral. We might relate this to the argument of both Goody (1977) and Ong (1958) that in Europe there was a major orientation to visual presentation that developed as a result of widespread literacy in the period following printing. We ultimately may want to relate the visual orientation of our role expectations to our literacy and the modern consciousness and to see the behavioral orientation to role expectations of thematic abstraction by contrast as multimodal.

These role expectations were found throughout the community of Fort Chipewyan. On the way to the store one day Rachel picked up a hockey puck that was lying on the ground. At the store a six year old girl saw her with it and began teasing her, "She's using boys' things." When our son was born, one ten year old said to R. Scollon that in ten years he would be living like a king because the boy would be chopping wood for him and everything. It is interesting in this case that this girl knew us well and knew that we lived where we had no need to chop wood. She was not referring to anything specific in our situation. She was characterizing the role relationship of a father and a son.

In another situation CB came into the house with a new music box. S. Scollon had seen his father at the store and asked if he had bought him the music box. CB's answer was,

| Daddy | "Daddy" |
| moose kaya. | "he went for moose" |

As a literal statement this was simply false. CB's father had not gone out hunting moose. He was in town and CB had not mistaken that. What he was saying in this case is that it was his father's role to hunt, not to buy toys at the store. That is what his mother and older sisters would do. His statement about his father's hunting is much like his handing R. Scollon a pen. It is a parsimonious statement of a role expectation. As an answer to a question it is not direct. It is the role that answers the question, not the speech. What CB had said identified the appropriate role expectation or theme from which the listener could understand the answer.

In looking back now at the first example we can see that a gesture, pointing to the seat in the study, the word "here," and the phrase "Daddy wé" are functional equivalents. While they may appear to be simple directives, we feel treating them as directives misses the point. We feel that CB was saying something more like "I've identified your role. It is sitting at that desk." The implication "Get back to it," is only indirectly a result of the assumption that individuals will act out their roles. By thematically abstracting one's role and by making reference to it one further places the obligation of conforming to it. It is the role placing the obligation, however, not the speaker. CB is not taking what for him would be an enormous liberty in telling an adult what to do. He is identifying the role and questioning one's right to step out of it. We see these role expectations as one way in which themes are abstracted out of the flux of knowledge. These themes group things into sets of predictable relationships. Here the relationships are among behaviors.

We can now see how to compare these role expectations with the decontextualization of literacy. We have argued that in the literate orientation there is a significant fictionalization of the self in the fictionalization of authorship. There is a heightened contextualization of the self through a fictionalization of the context in this case. From the literate point of view the self becomes a fiction in the role of the author, in the role of the reader, and in the extreme case of autobiography, even in the role of character. Distance is taken from the self. The self is projected as an object among objects in the world. Primary relationships are those within the text, not those between the text and the world.

We also see an important fictionalization from the point of view of thematic abstraction. The self is seen as deeply grounded in a context of predictable behaviors. The distance that can be taken from the view of the self is highly limited by a set of role expectations. The self in this case is not directly fictionalized. It is the context that is a fiction. As father, CB's father is a moose hunter. That is sufficient to explain why he could not have bought CB a music box and anyone would know that. All that needs to be pointed out is the role. The self from this point of view is highly contextualized within a role and distance from the role is circumscribed by convention and constant reminders.

Situational Chunking

Another way in which themes are abstracted is in viewing situations. Situations are regarded as complexes of predictable elements and expectations for the behavior of the individuals who are participants. One such situation for CB was glossed by him as "see-saw." Just outside our trailers was a small playground in which there were see-saws. CB and Rachel and the COS's often played there. CB referred to this whole situation as "see-saw." We feel that it is better to understand his use of "see-saw" as a metonym for the theme of playing in the playground than to seek to isolate in each use a different pragmatic function. In some cases "see-saw" meant something like "Let's go out and play." In others it meant something like "We've been outside." In still others it became much harder to interpret. He would say it while playing inside and showing no evidence of wanting to go out. He would say it even though they played outside without playing on the see-saws. We prefer a more indirect interpretation of pragmatic functioning in this case. We see the term "see-saw" as a metonym for the theme of playing. It is the theme then that takes on a pragmatic function. The theme in every case means a group of concepts including "I like to play in the playground. I like the see-saw. COS takes me out to play. COS puts me up and down on the see-saw," and so forth. A thematic mention, a metonymical reference, is sufficient to indicate all of these meanings. It is then up to the caregivers to decide what their role in this theme will be at that time. We see this metonymical reference to the theme as a highly developed mechanism for pragmatic indirectness. To the extent the theme has been accurately abstracted and there is general social agreement on this, the behavior of the participants is practically inevitable. The child who is in a way powerless to direct those in a superordinate position can by metonymical reference to these situational themes remind his superordinates of their caregiving duties. It is of course up to them to decide to what extent they will cooperate with culturally given expectations. It is not the child who directs but the society.

If we recall the example narrative in chapter five, we see a similar case. The spokesman, who is of course the leader of the group, expresses his desire to gather with the other group. He has no need to say it more directly since his suggestion will be followed. It is the social agreement among autonomous individuals that governs actions, not the intervention of one individual in the activities of another.

Another metonym for a theme which CB had abstracted was his "truck hidais!" This had other forms among which was "kádidáis." The literal meaning is something like "Truck one goes" or more colloquially "The truck (or car) goes." This metonym referred to a theme centering around but not restricted to riding in our car. CB often said this and we took it as requesting a ride in the car. He did not stop saying it, however, when we were in the car. He also frequently said it only in reference to the car or even in playing with a toy motorcycle. Again we feel that his use can best be understood by treating the actual forms said as references to the theme which is a complex of behavioral and situational elements. The exact pragmatic functioning of the utterance in any particular case is the result of an interaction between the set of expectations associated with the theme and the ongoing situation.

. Another theme that CB frequently referred to could be glossed in English as "shopping." CB's Chipewyan forms were "nahni" or "aɬni" and appeared in forms such as "mama kandis nahni" ("Mommy bought candies"), "ahkím ahni" ("someone bought ice cream"), "aɬni, aɬni, ejez aɬni" ("buy, buy, eggs buy"). As in the case of the other themes, CB was glossing a whole set of activities. In some cases this was done when someone returned from the store. In other cases it was when someone was going to the store. New objects were also thematized in this way. CB and his sisters also played at shopping.

This latter situation perhaps shows more clearly the difference between CB's thematic abstraction and Rachel's incipient literacy. We have quoted Rachel as saying "Chuck, chuck, chuck, that's what the knife said to the onion" (see chapter four). For her, even inanimate objects like the knife and onion could take on speaking roles in the fictionalization that comes with written narrative. For

CB just the opposite was observed. CB took on the role of the groceries in the "nahni" theme. He was often carried around in a paper bag as his sisters played out the shopping theme. His participation in the shopping theme was so complete that he could internalize the role of inanimate objects. Where Rachel animated objects into speech, CB inanimated himself as an object.

ROLES AND SITUATIONS AS THEMES

We do not see any important distinction between roles and situations from the point of view of thematic abstraction. What we see as critical is the abstraction of themes from the continuum of knowledge. The Chipewyan chief, Fred Marcel, spoke to us in reference to his life story. He said that one did not remember everything. That would be too much. He said that when a situation had passed, one thought back over it and remembered what was important. Afterwards the important details would never be forgotten and one would not be concerned about the other details. We see this as a statement of the principle of thematic abstraction by which skilled narrators create interactive stories. One selects out behaviors and events, characterizes them and then remembers them as units. We believe this ability to be well developed by Athabaskans and a central trait of the bush consciousness.

In a less mature example, COS was writing a story that S. Scollon was dictating to her. The story was a fiction but on the whole S. Scollon was dictating it according to Chipewyan narrative canons. One of these is that characters in a story who start out somewhere in the beginning must return home. This cycle constitutes a narrative theme that is violated only at the risk of unintelligibility. As they neared the end of the story S. Scollon said, "Then CB and Rachel fought until they killed each other. The end." As author she did not bring CB and Rachel, the central characters, home. COS said, "What, I can't even tell what you said!" S. Scollon repeated the ending. COS then said as she wrote, "Then CB and Rachel got to their home. The end." She would simply not accept a variation on a traditional theme. It is interesting to us that she characterized the variation as being beyond her perceptual ability. She did not say she would not write it. She said she could not even tell what had been said.

THEMATIC ABSTRACTION AND LANGUAGE

We have suggested and we will further develop the idea that the relationship between language and thematic abstraction is metonymical. By this we mean that an apt reference to a theme will abstract some characteristic and by referring to that characteristic refer to the whole theme. Succinctness is valued and no attempt is made to develop a full, explicit statement. These metonymical references may be thought of as indexing themes, not objects, persons, specific behaviors, or specific actions.

It is important to understand that we do not wish to suggest that language used in this sense is more or less "concrete" than in literate uses. It is differently contextualized. Where in literate uses of language the text becomes the central orientation, in thematic abstraction the theme is the focus. Literacy decontextualizes language by cutting it off from indexical references to situations. Writing itself becomes the context. In thematic abstraction what is decontextualized through fictionalization is the situation or role, that is, the theme. Language is highly contextualized through metonymy in themes, but the themes are decontextualized.

LINGUISTIC STRUCTURE AS METONYMY

We would like to argue that this relationship of metonymy applies as well to the grammatical system of Athabaskan. It has been known for years that linguists have not adequately dealt with the Athabaskan verb. Until recently we have not had an adequate way of understanding it. It has been known that the Athabaskan verb consists of a stem and some number of prefixes. The problem has been to assign a semantic role to the morphemes that can in many cases be easily identified on structural grounds. It has proved to be largely impossible to assign a single meaning to any morpheme that would hold up either comparatively throughout Athabaskan or even throughout various uses within a single language. The breakthrough in this work has come in the work of Kari and Leer in Alaska (Kari 1979, Leer 1979), who have begun looking at Athabaskan verbs in terms of themes. They have characterized various themes such as motion, operative, successive, conversive, stative, classificatory and descriptive. These themes are structural-semantic groupings of co-occurrences among paradigmatic stem sets, suffixes, and prefixes. The meanings of the verbs are in these themes, not in the elementary morphemic units out of which the themes are structurally composed. Kari and Leer have found in fact that the only way in which a successful meta-language for taking about Athabaskan verb structure could be developed was by creating a set of metonymical expressions by which they could refer to thematic co-occurrences.

As we have recently begun to look into the early work of Sapir on Athabaskan through the class notes of his students, we have begun to see that he had also understood the thematic nature of the Athabaskan verb. It is also easier now to see why he wrote so little about it. Where the ideal reference is metonymical it is very difficult to develop explicit, essayist descriptions of the same phenomenon. Kari and Leer have felt as Sapir undoubtedly did that a more indirect way of explicating Athabaskan verb structure is in keeping with the phenomenon.

We have wondered how a child could learn to speak Athabaskan in light of this problem. If one needs to know the full set of paradigmatic choices in the prefix system, the stem system, and the suffix system and the co-occurrences among them to express a common theme, how could a child possibly get all of this in mind before saying anything? The answer we would like to suggest is that the child does just what linguists did. The child begins with highly metonymical expressions, basically the stems, which refer to the verb theme in question without the additional requirement of being specific and explicit. In the early days of Athabaskan linguistics it was common to publish stem lists (Li 1933) with glossing statements that indicated that there was much more to the verb meaning than the stem. The stems indicated the range of meanings that were possible but for more specific semantics one would have to look at the prefix co-occurrences. We will show in the way that CB began to speak Chipewyan that he also took this same path into the complexity of verb themes.

The Peg Prefix Solution

Li (1946) identified a "peg" prefix on the verb which occurs in the position immediately preceding the classifier when there is no other required. CB used this peg prefix as his solution to the problem of representing that the verb theme consisted of a stem choice in co-occurrence with other prefix choices. As a first example we can look at the verb for "eating." As essential elements there are the thematic prefix cɛ́- and the stem -tɨ̵ (-tɨ̵ in the inceptive). Together these form the meaning encoded in English as "to eat." For CB this form was found as follows:

a. cɪtɨ̵   (asking to eat)

b. Rachel hitɨ̵   (Rachel is eating)
    Rachel hitɨ̵

c. hɪctɨ̵   (CB is eating)
    hɪctɨ̵

d. cɪ́tɨ̵   (urging Rachel to finish so they
    cɪ́tɨ̵   can go out to play)
    Rachel eat
    Rachel eat

The thematic prefix cɛ́- occurs only in **a** and in **d**. In **b** and **c** where there are person references the peg prefix hi is used. In **b** the person reference is a full nominal reference and in **c** it is the first person singular subjective prefix c, a phonetic variant of the normal s. The usual forms for **b** and **c** are "Rachel cɛ́tɨ̵ ("Rachel is eating") and "cɛ́stɨ̵" ("I am eating"). It seems reasonably clear from this and the following examples that CB has an overall restriction on the number of elements that can appear within a phrase. This limitation could be summarized as follows:

$$\left\{ \begin{matrix} & \text{thematic prefix} \\ & \text{peg prefix + person pronoun} \\ \text{subject noun +} & \text{peg prefix} \end{matrix} \right\} \;\; + \;\; \text{stem}$$

In every case the verb consists of two syllables at this stage.

These examples are marked for tone but we do not feel that we have good evidence that these pitches are significant. The high tones on the stem in **a** and **c** seem to be associated with first person but this is not confirmed by other examples. We do not have enough examples to establish any regular tonal system.

The general rule we have shown above can be seen again in the verb for "looking" as in the following examples.

a. nɛʔɨ̵   (showing tattoo on forehead)

b. kɪ́ hɨ̵ʔɨ̵   (showing a key)
    kɪ́ hɨ̵ʔɨ̵

c. hiʔiθ   (pushing Rachel back away from the baby)
    hiʔiθ
    hiʔiθ
    lʌk
    hiʔiθ
    (a bit later)
    hį̓ʔį

"You look" would normally be nį̓ɬʔį. In **a** CB shows the thematic prefix nɛ- which may be related to the word for "eye." Notice that this form does not have the nasalized vowel į which would indicate the second person singular "You." It is the thematic prefix plus the stem.

In **b** where there is a direct object, "key," CB uses the peg prefix, not the thematic prefix, and it does show nasalization for the second person singular. Again, as in the forms for the verb "to eat" the choice of a thematic prefix precludes marking for person. The choice of the peg prefix allows person marking in the verb.

In the example given in **c** there is neither a thematic prefix nor person marking. This may perhaps be explained by the fact that in this case the possibilities are considerable. Generally a postpositional phrase is closely associated with this theme which at a minimum could require two syllables in addition to some other thematic element. There is no clear, single thematic prefix as in the case of "looking" or "eating."

It is interesting to notice CB's use of an English word in this Chipewyan warning to step back. CB may have chosen the English "look" rather than the Chipewyan "hį̓ʔį" because of the phonetic similarity of the Chipewyan form with the form he used for "you'll kick." Since he used this Chipewyan form just a few minutes later it is clear that he knows how to use it. His choice of English seems motivated by an interest in phonetic clarity where his Chipewyan system has been considerably reduced by his use of the peg prefix in so many cases.

This use of the peg prefix was quite general. In the example given above, "truck hidais," CB again uses the peg prefix hi- where there is a nominal reference in the same clause. We also have nágis for "wide-eyed opening of the eyes" with only a thematic prefix and a stem, and ka híya the "the car went" with a nominal reference and a peg prefix.

The most extreme example of CB's use of the peg prefix was in his word hɛsbau for "baseball." In this case he treats "ball" as the stem, s as a person prefix and under the principle given above then uses the peg prefix. Presumably he could also say beibau if he eliminated the s element and analyzed the first syllable as a thematic prefix. We do not know to what extent CB knew other terms such as "basketball" or "volleyball" which would be logical sources of this analysis. We believe his analysis in this case to be more structural than semantic. This seems to be a matter of analogical development on the basis of the Chipewyan first person singular forms.

At this same time CB's possessive nouns had no prefixes. In Chipewyan a word such as "father" has an obligatory possessive prefix. "My father" would be sɛtá (from sɛ "my" tá "father"). CB in these cases used the noun stems freely without prefixes. We could generalize then and say that at this stage CB had at least two word classes, nouns and verbs. Nouns were free stems without prefixes, verbs were stems with a single syllable prefix, either a thematic prefix or a peg prefix with person marking in some cases.

It has been well established by now in the literature on child language that for many children there appears to be a limit on the amount of information that can be explicitly represented within a single phrase or tone group (Scollon 1976a, Brown 1973). Progression in the early stages appears as a successive inclusion of more elements within the tone group. We saw in CB's case just this progression with the qualification that CB marked a distinction between nouns and verbs, as we have said above. That is, we could not phrase this limit as an absolute limit on syllables or morphemes. With verbs there were two syllables as the limit within the verb and with nouns there was only a single syllable.

It is dramatic then to see that just when CB was able to program both a person marking and a thematic prefix within the same tone group he was also able to include the possessive prefix on possessed nouns. The limit went up by one in both cases to maintain the distinction between nouns and verbs.

We have in this period then forms such as the following:

```
Rachel sleeping
Rachel sleeping
Rachel θɛtį˙
Rachel θɛtį˙
```

In the second pair person is marked with "Rachel." There is also the thematic or conjugation marker θε as well as the stem tɨ'. At this same period CB began to say things such as [nič ʌk] "nitruck," that is, "your truck," with a clearly marked second person singular possessive prefix.

We could sketch out CB's development then in the following way:

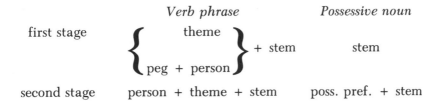

	Verb phrase	*Possessive noun*
first stage	$\left\{ \begin{array}{c} theme \\ peg + person \end{array} \right\}$ + stem	stem
second stage	person + theme + stem	poss. pref. + stem

It appears then that CB's solution to the problem of the complexity of the Athabaskan verb is to pick out from the verb theme essential elements which will be sufficient to index the correct verb theme. He even appears to have some hierarchical ordering among elements. The stem is always present. Next in importance is person marking, since this appears to override thematic marking. Next after person marking are thematic prefixes in the disjunct position. We do not have sufficient material to trace developments any more closely than this but it seems clear from our material that CB's metonymical peg prefix solution is the only possible one that is consistent with both quite general restrictions on the amount of information that young children can program into a single tone group and with the need to explicitly index situational and role themes.

The Vertical Construction

We would like to turn to more complex constructions involving several words. For some time it has been observed that many children in the period before they use two words together within a single tone group are able to make some kind of a meaningful sequence of words, each within its own tone group (Brown 1973, Bloom 1973, Scollon 1976a). Two things have been at issue. The first is the question of how representative of children this is. It is clear from Peters' (1977) work that many children do not use this strategy in learning languages. The second issue is the question of what these pre-syntactic sequences represent as linguistic constructions. Scollon (1976a) argued that these constructions, which he called vertical constructions, were based in the discourse patterns of interaction between the child and the caregiver and that these were the foundation on which syntax was based. Bloom (1973) also recognized the importance of these sequences but did not feel that they were in themselves syntactic. Now in chapter four we have argued that these vertical constructions are a crucial aspect in the early preparation for literacy. We feel that the central function of the interactive vertical construction is to provide the mechanism by which the caregiver can request the child to upgrade the information content of his or her utterance.

The typical vertical construction consists of a single utterance by the child, a request for new information by the caregiver, usually an adult, and then a comment by the child. The example given below is from Scollon (1976a) and repeated from chapter four:

Child: Kimby
Mother: What about Kimby?
Child: Close.

This question which asks "what about?" is the crucial fulcrum on which the building function of the vertical construction balances. As the child's ability progresses, more is built into the same tone group as the example below shows (also from Scollon 1976a):

Child: Tape recorder
use it
use it
Int: Use it for what?
Child: talk
corder talk
Brenda talk

The question we would like to address in looking at CB's development is whether or not he and his caregivers use vertical constructions and if so for what purposes they use them. There are a number of good examples in the material we have, some of which have been given above.

a. aɬni   buy
   aɬni   buy
   ɛjɛz aɬni   eggs buy

b. ahkím   ice cream
    ahni   buy
c. nič∧k   your truck
    nits∧k   your truck
    hílε   not
    nič∧k   your truck
    hiyâ·   went
d. ka   car
    hiya   went
e. Daddy   Daddy
    moose kaya   went for
                   moose

Except for the fact that these are all or in part in Chipewyan they look very much like the vertical constructions reported elsewhere (Scollon 1976a). Some, **a** and **c**, have repetitions and most (except a) are topic-comment sentences. **b**, **c**, **d**, and **e** are very much like normal Chipewyan sentences. There are two problems, however, with considering these to be the same phenomenon. The first is that overall they are very rare in CB's or other Athabaskan children's speech. It is much more common for sequences of CB's words not to add up informationally. That is, if he puts words into a sequence it seems preferable to see them as referring to isolated aspects of the situation rather than trying to put together an informationally coherent propositional statement.

The second problem is that we have never observed these vertical constructions to be interactive. We have no example in which the speech of another speaker intervened even accidentally between the separate parts of CB's constructions. We recognize that there is a significant possibility that this could have occurred in other contexts. CB was a visitor in our house where these records were made and so they were situationally quite different from the recordings made in R. Scollon's earlier work. Nevertheless, from the many cases in which COS did respond to CB in the same situation, and from cases we have observed in other contexts, we believe we can infer that the absence of interaction here was the usual practice. What then can we make of CB's vertical constructions? Formally they are very much as they should be. But they are rare and noninteractive.

We feel that it is better to see CB's vertical constructions as complex metonyms for situations or themes. We feel they reflect a different kind of decontextualization by comparison with other children who use this pattern. The vertical constructions used by other children become essentially narrative. In many cases they set up and develop accounts of events that are not present directly in the ongoing situation. Scollon found them to be most frequent in situations where the child was reading a book together with an adult. It is this sort of literate or narrative decontextualization that characterizes other children's vertical constructions. It is toward this literate use of language that other caregivers are drawing their children.

What is decontextualized with CB is not the narrative account of past or fictional events but rather the ongoing situation. All of the examples we have given above were given earlier as examples of metonymical references to themes. If we look back now at **a** and **b** we may recall that these index the theme of "shopping." CB uses these vertical constructions to typify the ongoing situation as an example of the shopping theme.

The examples given as **c** and **d** can be compared with the example given above, "truck hidais." Recall that that theme involved going in the car and all of the related activities. In the spring we had shipped the car out of Fort Chipewyan on the barge. This involved packing up things in the car, taking it down to the dock, negotiating with the barge company, waiting for several days as they unloaded and reloaded the barges, and watching the barges go. CB had been watching most of this activity with COS and his theme "ka hiya" or nitruck hiya" or "nitruck hílɛ" can be seen as indexing this whole package of several days' activity. The theme "ka hiya" replaced the theme "truck hidais" and we feel it was this quite abstract conceptualization that is represented in CB's vertical construction.

We have already discussed the example given in **e** above. CB was not saying that his father had gone hunting as would be the case in the more transparently narrative vertical constructions of other children we have observed. He was saying something about role expectations. He was saying that his father did not buy the music box. It will be recalled that this vertical construction was said in answer to a question about who had bought CB a new toy, not about where his father was. The answer was relevant and to the point but it was indirect in that it indexed a theme of role expectations. This is the sense in which we say that CB's vertical constructions are decontextualized but in a different way from the narrative decontextualization we had come to expect.

We see this difference in vertical construction relating to the difference observed in chapter five between the Athabaskan stanza and the English stanza. There we argued for a pervasive ordering of action before explanation for Athabaskans and the reverse order for English. Now we have seen that the vertical construction calls for an ordering of expectation followed by action. In this is it incompatible with the ordering of the Athabaskan stanza and so it is not surprising to see that these are quite rare with CB.

CODE SWITCHING

In the examples we have now given we have seen words in English and words in Chipewyan. We would now like to consider whether or not CB, who is learning both languages, does any code switching and if so for what purposes he does it. Words such as "nitruck" ("your truck") suggest that the English morpheme "truck" is being treated as borrowed since it can take the Chipewyan possessive prefix. If that were the case then the earlier use of "truck" in "truck hidais" might also be regarded as borrowed and this would be a fully Chipewyan phrase. And the form for "baseball", hɛsbau, has been structurally modified very much along the lines of a Chipewyan verb at that stage for CB. It would seem on the basis of these forms that CB does not really separate Chipewyan and English into separate codes. He appears to be treating all words in the environment within one grammatical and phonological system and that is very much like Chipewyan.

We have seen one example in which CB made an obvious choice between two alternate forms, "look" and " hį́ʔį ." There we suggested that his choice was made in order to provide structural clarity. He chose the English form not to be speaking English but because it contrasted more strongly with the preceding and following " hiʔiθ ." An example like this would suggest to us that CB knew there were alternate ways in which things could be said and that he made his choice out of a motivation of structural contrast.

A number of examples lead us to believe that CB did have an awareness that some people did not speak both languages. In speaking to us or our daughter he often covered the ground by saying everything twice in both languages. Sometimes these would be mixed within a tonal group as in

```
kusígal cóme          "Come!"
kusígal cóme
```

and in other cases they would be separated as in

```
cítį                  "Eat!"
cítį

Rachel eat
Rachel eat.
```

In at least one situation which will be detailed below CB registered surprise at one of us saying something to him in Chipewyan.

It is difficult then to establish just what awareness CB had of English and Chipewyan as distinct codes. Structurally he did not make any strong distinctions. In regard to some speakers he seemed to feel that things in Chipewyan might not be understood. What we would like to point out now is that in the function of indexing themes he seemed to make no distinction between languages. We would suggest that the themes that CB and others had constructed were independent of any particular language. That is, one could refer to the same theme in either language or both.

THE INITIATION OF INTERACTION

We have said that for CB the vertical construction was not interactive. Now we would like to look more generally at several situations to discuss the ways in which CB did initiate interactions with other people.

In one case CB kept darting up to R. Scollon and Rachel and touching them. As he touched them he said "kú" and then ran away. This morpheme, if it must be glossed, means "then." It normally has very little specific meaning. In most cases in ordinary conversation it is used to indicate a shift in pragmatic function. In narratives it is used to mark episodic boundaries (see chapter five). CB's use in this case appeared to be related to these in that he was trying to get attention or initiate some kind of interaction.

In another case he went up to R. Scollon and showed him his hand which had been blackened from some carbon paper he had been playing with. R. Scollon said "nila delzen" ("your hand is black"). CB smiled and started to walk away. After two steps he stopped short, turned around and looked at R. Scollon in amazement. This was the first he had heard him use any Chipewyan. After that he searched around the house bringing things to hand silently to R. Scollon to encourage him to keep talking.

This silent initiation of interactions is strikingly different from the child Scollon (1976a) observed who by two years of age had learned to control topics in interactions with adults by controlling initiations. Schegloff (1972) had observed that conversations were opened with summons-answer sequences in which the original summoner asked for the right to speak, the answerer granted that right, and the original speaker then introduced the topic. The two-year-old in R. Scollon's study had learned that by handing an object and saying "here" she could control the introduction of the topic. She used this as a strategy for limiting conversations with adults to topics over which she had lexical or structural control. Where another speaker sought to initiate an interaction with her she would interrupt by handing him an object and then go on as if the conversation had been at her initiative.

CB's initiations were puzzling to us in light of these previous studies and our own expectations. He would initiate an interaction but then appear to abdicate any claim to control the interaction. It was our expectation that a minimal response from us would be sufficient for him to take the floor and speak. He did not do this. He seemed to expect us to speak.

A second observation confirms that this is in fact what CB expected. When we asked people how to initiate conversations they always told us to say " ?ɛdlánɛt'ɛ" "how are you?" When we asked what the appropriate answer was, they would say it was "?ɛsǫ́st'ílɛ" "I'm fine" or more literally "It is nothing to me." Then somewhere later in the discussion they would say you should say "?ɛdlánɨ̃ðen" ("what do you think?"). When we asked what the answer to that was, they always said that the correct answer was whatever you thought. That is, this initiation was completely open to the initiative of the answerer, not the questioner. This initiation bothered us for two reasons. The first was that our Chipewyan was not good enough to be able to come up with much to say. The second was really probably more important. Because of our own social norms of conversational interaction we felt that the questioner should take the responsibility in controlling topic. We should be provided with some formulas by which to respond adequately, not with open-ended opportunities to speak.

Our observations in the community indicate that this latter initiation is in fact the norm. The first initiation we were told is really a calque on the English or French pattern. People expected us to want that sort of initiation and gave it to us. We rarely heard it used by anyone except in speaking to us and then one felt it was being done for display. Interactions were usually more like the following:

ʔɛdlánɛt'ɛ	"How are you?"
ʔɛsóst'ílɛ	"I'm fine."
ʔɛdlánįðen	"What do you think?"
Ummm.	"Ummm."

In consideration of this pattern of interaction in the community we can understand that CB's initiations are entirely consistent. His initiations were intended to get us to talk, not to talk himself. If we recall what we have said earlier about the relationship of dominance and display we can see that some such mechanism is necessary if the child is to get the necessary linguistic input to be able to learn. Where the superordinate member of a pair is expected to speak and the subordinate member is expected to be reserved in speaking it would be difficult for a child to engage in interactions with adults without violating this cultural norm. If the child can initiate interactions without the expectation that the one who initiates must control the topic, the child has a mechanism by which he can show his willingness to listen to the talk of adults. We feel this interaction pattern is a necessary concomitant of the linkage of dominance and display for Chipewyans. It is an integral part of a system of nonintervening social interaction.

TRAINING FOR THEMATIC ABSTRACTION

Now that we have begun to discuss interaction patterns we can look more closely at how children are taught to abstract themes and to refer to them metonymically. We have argued that thematic abstraction is a means by which knowledge is organized. This organization shows up in narrative performances as well as in their recall and comprehension. This organization is based on general schemata or themes which are of at least two types, situational themes and role expectation themes. We feel that it is fair to consider these themes to be a means of decontextualization of situations and behaviors. Human variability is organized around typifications and the typifications further are taken as norms for behavior. One of the principal uses of language is to refer to these themes. This reference is essentially indexical, not explicit. It is metonymical in that some key element of the theme is taken as representing the whole theme. Much of what is said may be thought of as metonymical indexing of these themes. Speech does not refer to specific elements of situations, contexts, or behaviors. The learning of thematic abstraction then can be thought of as consisting of three aspects—learning themes, learning decontextualization of the self from situations toward contextualization in culturally determined roles, and learning metonymical indexing of themes.

Themes

We have already seen several examples in which a child was being instructed in appropriate themes. When COS held her hand before an infant's eyes to prevent him from exchanging glances with his father she was instructing him in an appropriate relationship with his parents. In some cases the instruction was more explicit, as in the situation when COS told CB to go do man's work. The play among CB and his two COS's, where CB was the groceries in the shopping theme, shows the extent to which CB was able to internalize themes.

Narratives play an essential part in the instruction of themes. This instruction begins by modeling listening. With a very young infant everything is taken as meaningful. Any shake of the head or movement of the shoulders is taken as expressing something to which the adult responds. The cooing [gɨ] was taken as "gu" or "guwaze" ("worm" or "little worm"). The adult or caregiver asks the infant questions and then any response is taken as the answer. In this way the older speakers show listening patterns to the child.

These same infants are told stories and made to be quiet and pay attention. These stories are of course much beyond the comprehension of the infants and young children at first but the picking out of bits and pieces of understanding is taken as the first step toward thematic abstraction.

Decontextualization of Self

We want now to look at ways in which children are taught to step out of the current situation into a more decontextualized view of the self and their own participation in social events. The first element of this training is the development of a sort of stoicism. Children are teased in various ways. CM called our infant son a "little skunk" and said that she had teased her own children in the same way. As children grow older, adults and especially other children tease them until they learn to accept this teasing without crying or even without overt signs of annoyance.

One case in which several children teased our two-year-old daughter Rachel was both descriptively and symbolically revealing. First they began to taunt her until she got irritated. Then when she acted as if she might cry they said they were going to throw her in a trash can. That made her cry. They then began to tease her about crying. They said her parents were going to go away and leave her because of her crying, that parents did not tolerate crying babies. Then finally this tormenting reached its symbolic height when they pretended to steal her face and throw it away. Rachel took this all quite literally and claimed that she needed her face and they could not have it.

What is striking to us in this example is the quite explicit message that for one to be able to keep one's face one has to renounce the fear of losing it. By ignoring these torments Rachel soon learned to keep her composure and in doing so to keep her face. It was by treating these immediate, physical, and situationally real threats as nonexistent that Rachel began to learn how to remove herself from situations. This decontextualization treats the role as primary. The role is the context in which one behaves, not the actual situation.

At the other extreme from teasing is the indifference to children's speech and behavior that people display. There is little middle ground. On the one hand children are teased into silence. On the other hand their speech is frequently ignored. It is not totally ignored, but a child in speaking can have no confidence that his speech will be treated as pragmatically grounded in the ongoing speech event.

The preschool at Fort Chipewyan employs several visiting

teachers from the community. These teachers are supposed to make home visits in order to prepare the children for attendance at the preschool by first getting acquainted with Indian teachers in the house. The two women who visited Rachel and CB most often would display some game or toy for Rachel to play with. From then on they would talk to each other and almost completely ignore anything Rachel said. On one occasion as Rachel played with a doll she began by saying "Nice dolly," and looking at the teachers for some response. She got no response and tried again. She kept this up for some fifteen to twenty times and then finally trailed off into a musical chant. Her pragmatic conversational work had been turned into a theme of child's play by this careful ignoring of her speech.

In another case Rachel's questions were turned back by COS in a narrative frame. COS worked up a story in which "big mouth Mother Goose" was destroyed because she asked too many questions.

We have used mostly examples from our daughter because by the time we met CB he had already been well socialized into these patterns of discourse. Rachel in the view of COS and others in the community had a long way to go and they seriously undertook her instruction. As time passed she in fact became behaviorally much like CB in contexts of play with him and his family.

It has often been observed that Athabaskans indulge their children. Except for the specific cases of teasing that we have mentioned, children are allowed a very wide range of behavior. Only actions that might result in serious physical damage are prevented. Minor damages such as the burns that might develop from touching a stove are usually taken as less serious than interfering in a child's behavior and a child is rarely told not to do something.

This indulgence is related to the decontextualization of self in several ways. In the first place, this indulgence is a necessary outcome of the relationship between dominance and display. We have said that the person in the subordinate position is expected to be the spectator and the person in the superordinate position is expected to display. It is necessary for the person in the superordinate position to ignore the behavior of the child in order to avoid an inversion of the relationship. Paying too much attention to the child would be tantamount to taking a spectator's role and to placing oneself in a position that is subordinate to the child. To insist on saying a particular thing or on behaving in a particular way would require the superordinate to keep checking on the child's behavior as a display of obedience. This threat to the dominant position can be avoided by ignoring the child's behavior.

A second way in which this indulgence relates to thematic abstraction is by modeling a role of indifference to the situation or to actual behavior. Themes are allowed to play themselves out without close intervention on the part of the participants. This shifts the focus away from the here and now onto a more abstract schema of situations, roles, or behaviors.

By creating a general background of noninterference in the child's behavior it is possible to focus teasing more sharply as the specific mechanism of training. Where the child expects noninterference and gets strong intervention instead we can suppose that this intervention is felt to be all the more significant.

The indulgence that COS shows CB can be seen in two examples. In the first case COS set out on a walk with us. CB was being kept home by his mother and began to cry. COS would not leave until CB stopped crying. Then after going a little distance she ran home again just to make sure CB had not started crying again.

At another time we were up on a hill looking through binoculars. CB was buzzing around R. Scollon who was looking through the binoculars. Because CB was pulling on his arm it became very difficult for R. Scollon to see anything. He asked CB to stop and CB started crying. COS then turned on R. Scollon and scolded him for being so insensitive to CB as to make him cry. This violation of CB's general indulgence was taken so seriously by COS that she was willing to speak harshly to an adult rather than allow it to go unnoticed. Of course R. Scollon was expected to indulge the ten year old scolding him as well.

We see teasing and noninterference as the two mechanisms by which children are trained in the decontextualization of self. This consists of a removal of the self from specific situations and behaviors into thematically typified situations and behaviors which are seen as the solid ground of reality.

Metonymical Indexing

The third aspect of thematic abstraction that a child needs to learn is how to index themes parsimoniously in speech. We are calling the basic mechanism metonymical because references select out some aspect of the whole theme for statement and in stating that aspect suggest the remaining theme. In order to understand this learning process we need to think for a moment about how children learn to mean (Halliday 1975). Without looking further into a child's motivation we can begin with the child speaking. Whatever it was the child had in mind to say or to do before speaking, it comes to have meaning in interaction with the interpretations placed on his speech by others in the social context. In this sense a child's speech means what it is taken to mean, not necessarily what it was intended by the child to mean. Halliday (1975) has shown how the earliest system the child uses is to a large extent invented by the child. As the interpreted meanings begin to be experienced by the child the child's system moves toward the environmental system which is usually the adult system. In Halliday's sense then meaning can be seen as socially constructed in interactions between the child and other speakers.

In the case of CB we have said that on the whole people do not respond to him, at least not directly. In the sense of meaning we have used above, then, CB does not mean anything when he speaks. That is, CB's speech has no interactive meaning. In order to understand just what kind of meaning CB's speech has we have to look a bit more closely at just how people react to his speech.

We have said that COS does not often respond to CB. What she does do much more often is talk about CB's speech. In many cases for us these look superficially like translations. CB would say, "nuhgal, nuhgal" and COS would say it means "Let's go home." Or CB would say "hɨyá" and COS would say it means "hurry up." These cases might lead one to believe that COS was translating except that she is not translating the meaning of the words but rather the meaning of the theme. The first means literally something like "We (pl) go (sg)" and the second means "You (sg) go (sg)." The meanings are close maybe but not exact.

In other cases though what CB said was in English and on the face of it perfectly interpretable to us.

gíšəm
gíšəm
gíšəm

was not hard to interpret as "Gimme some!" but COS duly said,

"He says, 'gimme some'." In another case CB came in and told us,

> bebi
>
> bebi
>
> toys
>
> toys
>
> toys
>
> look
>
> look

COS again glossed for CB by saying, "He's saying that because he went to see a baby."

The point we wish to make here is that rather than respond directly to CB's speech, what COS did was to gloss it thematically. She rarely took anything he said as situationally relevant. We feel she provided these glosses as a means of suggesting to CB that what he said could be taken as metonymically related to themes. In vertical constructions with other children the interlocutor, by asking the "so what?" question indicates to the child how the child may make the utterance interactionally relevant. COS, by talking about the meanings of CB's speech, models the indexing of themes at the same time she models a pattern of verbal indirectness in this case. We would argue that these indirect modeling statements are the mechanism by which CB was instructed in metonymical indexing.

The parallel between this interactive pattern and the riddle is obvious. One might say that COS takes CB's utterances as riddles which she guesses. As we recall the riddle-like aspect of the Athabaskan verse we can see in these interactions between COS and CB a preparation for the adult oral narrative interaction. Finally, the way in which COS glosses CB's utterances after the fact is consistent with the structure of the Athabaskan stanza in which action is followed by explanation, motivation or evaluation. In these interactions of COS and CB we can see the beginnings of the highly polished adult narrative performance.

We have sketched the outlines of a cognitive orientation which we are calling thematic abstraction. This orientation is learned early in life through a process of socialization to the linguistic and communicative patterns of the bush consciousness and is at the foundation of the intellectual capacities of maturity. We have contrasted thematic abstraction with literacy, especially essayist literacy as a means of highlighting differences. Now we would like to emphasize that in drawing these contrasts we do not intend to suggest that thematic abstraction is in some way a polar opposite to essayist literacy.

Goody (1977) has shown to what extent what we have called essayist literacy depends on lists and tables in cognitive organization. As an essay this chapter and indeed the entire book may too easily be understood by the reader as implying a binary set of oppositions, a two-column list. We do not mean to set up essayist literacy in one column and thematic abstraction in a second column and then compare them feature by feature down the rows. Contrasts do help to clarify differences but they do not necessarily imply a patterned set of relationships between the two phenomena so arrayed.

We do not know how many reality sets there are. We are sure there are more than two. Essayist literacy or the modern consciousness do not oppose thematic abstraction or the bush consciousness to close out the field of study. We also do not know to what extent either of these cognitive orientations is wholly exclusive of the other. We are not even sure what that would mean. Hymes (1966) has given us an important caution in his discussion of linguistic relativity. Presumably thematic abstraction learned early in life would affect one's overall thought processes in a more pervasive way than this same orientation learned later. The same is true of literacy. Do we know what possibilities there are for simultaneous early and profound development of both orientations? We suggest that we do not and as of this writing we would like to caution the reader that here we are typifying reality sets through what seem to be clear cases. Most cases are not so clear. We need to be careful not to mistake our theoretical constructs for the real thing.

PART THREE

FACE AND CULTURAL PLURALISM

SEVEN

DISCOURSE AS POLITENESS PHENOMENA

THE PROBLEM OF SOURCES

We have argued for two contrasting reality sets, the bush consciousness and the modern consciousness, each of which carries with it a typical pattern of interaction, the "English" discourse patterns and "Athabaskan" discourse patterns which we discussed beginning in chapter two. We have further identified these with what we have called essayist literacy on the one hand and the abstraction of themes on the other. In closing chapter six we cautioned against too easy an alignment of these in a six cell matrix. The matrix suggested may well be another product of essayist literacy, as Goody (1977) has cautioned us.

We will address the problem presented by the internal coherence of these patterns and reality sets in this chapter. The problem is one of determining the sources of these systems. Even if we grant the internal logic of the association of the modern consciousness, English discourse patterns, and essayist literacy, how is it to be explained that people come to know and manifest these systems? Surely each aspect is not learned or deduced separately and only then pieced together into a system. We argue that productive systems of cultural behavior are the result of the interaction of human universals and the culturally specific input of a particular group.

If we assume a set of communicative universals and a group of culturally specific inputs we still have the problem of determining the nature of both the universals and the specific inputs. The task in this case is to characterize a universal system such that given two different inputs the result will be the modern consciousness and its discourse patterns on the one hand and the bush consciousness and its discourse patterns on the other.

Here we will take up the suggestion of chapter six that for the bush consciousness a system of "face" is the governing universal system. We argued that a child being socialized to the bush consciousness had to give up the fear of losing face in order to keep face. This may be characterized as valuing "negative face," that is, the right to independence and autonomy. In discussing essayist literacy we argued that a key to understanding the system lay in the fictionalization of the self. This, again, we would argue amounts to a face consideration. In short, the communicative universals of concern in understanding both the bush consciousness and the modern consciousness are universals of face. What varies from system to system in both these and other systems is the nature of the "givens," the values placed on different aspects of face in a particular group. Given a difference in value, the set of face universals determines different communicative strategies.

UNIVERSALS IN LANGUAGE USAGE

Brown and Levinson (1978) have given us the outlines of a universal system of politeness phenomena. They have argued cogently that the amount of syntactic variability observed by linguists in the world's languages is elaborated beyond any conceivable referential or purely informational needs. They have argued that this variability can, however, be accounted for by viewing this variability as necessary for the management of face considerations in interpersonal communication. It is because of the need to delicately balance the degree or weight of communicative impositions on the hearer that such elaborate systems have developed. They have further shown that similar politeness or face strategies are employed in functionally similar ways in strikingly different societies. Whenever the same facework needs to be done, the means for doing it are very similar even in languages which are very different from each other structurally. Thus Brown and Levinson have suggested a universal system of politeness strategies that accounts for within-system structural variability by variable interactive needs within the system. Cross-system structural differences are accounted for by cross-system differences in interactional needs.

We believe that the problem we have outlined will be solved along the lines suggested by Brown and Levinson. In our discussion in this chapter we will rely quite heavily on their work. Our use of their work, however, extends beyond the level of the speech act to include the more global strategies of discourse and indeed whole communicative systems. Brown and Levinson themselves suggest this possibility but should not be held responsible for the use we make here of their suggestion. In short, partly on the basis of Brown and Levinson's work and partly by extension from it, we believe that variability in discourse patterns may be accounted for as variability in interactional needs.

In our discussion of Athabaskan oral narrative performances in chapter five we have already suggested, in fact, that the structure of the narrative was a product of the interactional and even face needs of storyteller and audience. Here we will tie this analysis more closely to a view of universals of interpersonal interaction.

Finally, a caution is necessary to understand our extension of Brown and Levinson's work. They discuss the structure of single speech acts. Even at the level of the speech act a single act may incorporate multiple face strategies. At the level of the discourse or above that at the level of the communicative system this mixing of strategies becomes the nature of the system. The face strategies that they outline are analyzed for single acts. We believe that these same strategies may be realized by whole discourses as well. We must, however, be careful not to fall into a problem of logical typing (Bateson 1979) in forgetting whether we are speaking of discourse which consists of multiple speech acts or, on the other hand, of single speech acts. Our emphasis in this discussion is on the discourse and even the whole communicative system. We assume any communication at that level to consist of a complex structure of many different interactional strategies encoded as speech acts.

FACE AND POLITENESS STRATEGIES

The basic assumption of a universal theory of face is that any act of communication is a threat to face, that is, to the public self-image that a person seeks to maintain. Face consists of two aspects, negative and positive face. Because face is the public self-image that the person seeks to maintain, the term "negative" is used to indicate a preferred withdrawal from the public or social world. "Positive" is used to indicate a preferred entrance into the social sphere. Brown and Levinson define negative face as

> The basic claim to territories, personal preserves, right to non-distraction, i.e. to freedom of action and freedom from imposition (p. 66).

They define positive face as

> The positive consistent self-image or "personality" (crucially including the desire that this self-image be appreciated and approved of) claimed by interactants (p. 66).

An act of communication threatens the hearer's negative face to the extent that it imposes on him and his right to autonomy, whether the imposition is one of expected behaviors or of ideas. It threatens the hearer's positive face to the extent that it suggests that the hearer does not want to be thought of well by others in some sphere of public activity. In this it can be seen that, in fact, to the extent that a communicative act is addressed to respect the hearer's negative face it may actually threaten his positive face. From this tension between negative and positive face comes the social necessity to seek a careful balancing of face in all communicative acts.

Because face is the public self-image claimed by participants, each participant has a vested interest in respecting the face wants of others. One who runs roughshod over the face wants of others may gain some degree of independence and autonomy but by his destruction of his interactant's face he loses the expectation of consideration in return. Face is granted to others in the expectation of a fair return and thus is the essence of social interaction. The persistent need for the balancing of individual and social needs is reflected in the concepts of negative and positive face.

Communicative acts may be arrayed on a scale from lesser to greater risk of loss of face. Some acts are scarcely a risk and may be done with little further consideration. Others are so grave that they may not be undertaken at all. The system of interest lies in between, acts that require a careful consideration of their face implications. Brown and Levinson's paper is largely taken up with an enumeration and description of communicative strategies that will produce acts of a calculated weight. What is of interest is the discussion of the overall system for our purposes. In their typology they give five possibilities from lesser to greater risk of face loss. The strategies are broadly characterized and grouped as (adapted from Brown & Levinson):

1. Bald on record
2. Positive politeness   } Solidarity
3. Negative politeness
4. Off record   } Deference
5. Not done

"Bald on record" strategies are undertaken with the least concern for face. These strategies are on record. That is, they are clearly impositions, taken to be impositions, and not mistaken as anything else nor ambiguous in any way. These strategies are only undertaken where there is little or no risk of the loss of face.

Also on record as impositions are the second and third groups, positive and negative politeness. Positive politeness addresses the hearer's positive face, that is, his desire to be approved of by others. Among the strategies used to communicate positive politeness Brown and Levinson give (1978:107, our numbering):

1. Notice, attend to H (his interests, wants, needs, goods)
2. Exaggerate (interest, approval, sympathy with H)
3. Claim in-group membership with H
4. Claim common point of view, opinions, attitudes, knowledge, empathy
5. Indicate S knows H's wants and is taking them into account
6. Assume or assert reciprocity

From these strategies can be seen the general nature of positive politeness in asserting common ground for both the speaker (S) and the hearer (H). The essence of positive politeness is the assertion of some underlying sameness between interactants. Being members of the same group usually reduces the weight of the imposition. Thus the assertion of some common group membership can be used as a strategy to reduce the overall weightiness of the imposition and the consequent risk to face.

It is interesting in this context to recall Erickson's (1976) finding that in gatekeeping encounters where access to movement in institutional power structure is controlled through the management of face-to-face interaction that it is co-membership that provides one of the two most serious "leakages." Co-membership of the interactants in gatekeeping encounters tends to provide improved access to the power structure to the outside party. We suggest that this is a reflection of the effect of positive politeness in reducing impositions and consequently the risk of face loss to the gatekeeper.

Negative politeness is addressed to the hearer's negative face, that is, his right to independence of activity and autonomy in relation to the relevant social sphere. The essence of negative politeness is deference. Among the strategies mentioned by Brown and Levinson are (1978:136, our numbering):

1. Make minimal assumptions about H's wants, what is relevant to H
2. Give H option not to do act
3. Minimize threat
4. Apologize
5. Dissociate S, H from the particular infringement
6. State the F(ace) T(hreatening) A(ct) as a general rule
7. Nominalize

Negative politeness acknowledges the seriousness of the imposition in the act of making it. While positive politeness is directed more to the general nature of the relationship between interactants, negative politeness is directed to the specific act of imposition. Even in this assumption that the particular act is what is of significance, negative politeness shows the general characteristic of not taking anything for granted about the wants or needs of the hearer, the one on whom one is imposing.

The fourth general strategy advanced by Brown and Levinson is going "off record." Where the risk is very great, the face threatening act is phrased in such a way that if necessary it could be taken as not having been an imposition at all. That is, off record strategies are ambiguous. Two meanings are presented giving the hearer the option of responding either to the imposition or to the surface value of the utterance.

More serious face threatening acts are not encoded at all. They are simply not said.

POLITENESS SYSTEMS

It seems intuitively clear that any regularly interacting system such as a group of professionals, an adolescent peer group, a classroom, a family, or a courtroom will develop some internal regularity in its interaction patterns. The politeness strategies exercised will tend toward regularity to the extent that face requirements are consistent within the system. Brown and Levinson suggest the possibility of characterizing overall systems as positive politeness systems or negative politeness systems.

Here we would prefer to introduce two terms not used by Brown and Levinson. We would prefer "solidarity politeness" where they use "positive politeness" and "deference politeness" where they use "negative politeness" to characterize global systems of politeness. We have two reasons. The first is to avoid a terminological confusion of global systems of politeness with the particular politeness strategies used. Our second reason is to avoid the negative evaluation of deference politeness that is suggested by the use of the term "negative." As we will argue, deference systems should be most highly valued in situations of communicative complexity.

A solidarity politeness system in this framework would favor low numbered strategies (bald on record and positive politeness) while a deference politeness system would favor higher numbered strategies (negative politeness, off record, or avoiding the face threatening act). The internal dynamics of a solidarity politeness system would favor the emphasis on sameness, of group membership, and the general good of the group. Deference politeness systems would favor deference, indirectness or even avoidance of making impositions on others at all.

These internal dynamics of deference and solidarity politeness systems give to them system properties of considerable interest. While Brown and Levinson say that face may only be given by speakers to hearers, not asserted by speakers in regard to themselves, we would suggest that positive and negative face are not alike in this respect. Because of the general assertion of sameness or commonality in solidarity politeness, any speaker using this strategy in regard to a hearer is simultaneously asserting it for himself. That is, solidarity politeness attends not only to the positive face of the hearer, it consolidates the positive face position of the speaker.

Negative face on the contrary only can be gained by the hearer at the speaker's loss. To the extent that I grant the freedom of unimpeded activity to my hearer I lose my own. To the extent I assert my own right to autonomy, my own negative face, I risk that of my hearer. This difference between negative and positive face and the corresponding politeness systems may be sketched out as below:

	speaker's negative face	speaker's positive face	hearer's negative face	hearer's positive face
deference politeness	−	−	+	−
solidarity politeness	−	+	−	+

Deference politeness as a system has a negative feedback loop built into it. In a deference politeness system the overriding value shared by all participantas is on negative face. The fact that the only means by which an individual can gain negative face is by having it extended to him by others, not by his own direct activities, means that one is careful to always respect the negative face of others. The individual's loss of negative face in granting it to others provides a control on the system to prevent either excessive loss or gain of negative face on any member's part.

Solidarity politeness systems, on the other hand, risk developing runaway positive feedback loops. Bateson (1972, 1979) has called this sort of system symmetrically schismogenic. That is, a schism is produced through a positive internal feedback loop that escalates the activity within the system until it falls apart. In a solidarity politeness system the overriding value for all members is on positive face. In granting positive face to my hearer I simultaneously assert it for myself. My hearer in return must grant me positive face and in order for it to be noticeable it must be granted with some increment of gain. At the same time he is increasing his own positive face. The system is in Bateson's (1979) term "addictive." The system thrives on more and more of the same. Some solidarity politeness begets more. Because both parties gain in the transaction there is no limit to runaway growth, to ever-increasing expression of commonality.

From the properties of the two systems then we can see that a deference politeness system tends toward resilience (Holling 1976). It is stable or resilient over time and many interactions. This is the resilience of the open, ecologically viable system (Prigogine 1976).

A solidarity politeness system, on the other hand, tends toward greater and greater closing of the system. Because of the ever-increasing expression of commonality, the solidarity politeness system ultimately places stress on all members' negative face wants. This condition of schismogenesis will ultimately result in the rupture of the system into smaller and separate groups within which some degree of negative face can be restored.

We suggest that solidarity politeness systems tend to be short-lived, rapidly escalating systems in which the shared goals, interests and attributes of members are emphasized while the differences among them are minimized in face-to-face expression. These systems tend toward increasing the expression of commonality and ultimately so minimize the difference among members that a need to break down the system is experienced because of negative face wants and new groups are formed.

Deference politeness systems tend to be much more stable over time and resilient in that the acceptance of outside influence is tolerated without major system stress. In these systems the differences among members are emphasized, the assumption is that one may not easily anticipate the needs or wants of others and any impositions are made in the context of careful respect for the right of the other to avoid imposition.

Sources of Politeness Systems

Brown and Levinson treat the weight of the imposition that causes risk of face loss as the sum of three factors, the power relationship between the participants (P), the distance between them (D), and the ranking or absolute weight of the imposition itself (R). The formula $W_x = P + D + R$ expresses this relationship among the three factors. As W_x increases a higher-numbered politeness strategy is used. Solidarity politeness strategies are used with relatively low values for W_x and deference politeness strategies are used with higher values. Since the weight (W) of the imposition (x) is a sum, it is possible to play each of the three factors off against each other in communication. This means that system needs can be played off against individual needs in the exchange of P, D, and R.

If for example the need were for a highly resilient system, high W_x values would produce the appropriate interactive strategies. This could be accomplished by either an increase of D or R or both. An increase in P tends to produce asymmetrical systems of deference politeness upward from the less powerful interactants and positive politeness or bald on record strategies downward from the more powerful interactants, as will be described later.

If on the other hand the need were for a closed, less stable system in which commonality of members was to be emphasized, giving P, D, and R low values would produce the necessary face strategies. As an example we can imagine situations in which a high amount of information needs to be exchanged over a relatively brief period. Because each act of information exchange would tend to produce R's of some value and many of these are expected, P and D would have to be kept at an absolute minimum. To insure the easy flow of information with minimum risk to face, a system of solidarity politeness would be needed. To do this the power differences and distances would have to be minimized among participants. It seems that academic conferences or adolescent peer groups approach this sort of situation.

Types of Politeness Systems

Brown and Levinson suggest at least three general types of systems based on values of power and distance. The first is asymmetrical because of a high value on differences of power ($+P$). Whether or not distance is regarded as great, these systems tend to use low numbered strategies downward and high numbered stratagies upward. That is, the member with the power ($+P$) orders and the other shows deference.

The other two systems are symmetrical. The power difference is assumed to be low ($-P$), that is, it is assumed that there is little difference in power between the participants. The actual power is not of relevance but the difference. The two systems differ on the value of distance. Where distance is assumed to be high ($+D$) a deference politeness system is the result because of the relatively high W_x values. Where distance is assumed to be low ($-D$), a solidarity politeness system is the result because of the relatively low W_x values.

These systems are sketched in the taxonomic chart below:

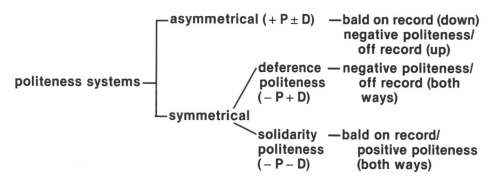

ATHABASKAN DISCOURSE PATTERNS
AS DEFERENCE POLITENESS

The essence of Athabaskan communicative style is respect for the autonomy and independence of other individuals. In terms of this study of face, Athabaskan communicative style is a deference politeness system. As we have just outlined, the crucial values are

a.   − P, an assumption of a low power difference between members

b.   + D, an assumption of a high distance between members

The nonintervention we have described for the bush consciousness is another wording for the assumption of high distance value. Nonintervention is paying respect to the negative face of other members and, as we have said, this respect for negative face can only be achieved reciprocally, not through self-assertion.

We argued in chapter five that the Athabaskan interactive narrative constituted a strategy for minimizing the threat of imposing one's view of the world on others. Now in the light of the politeness stratagies we have reviewed above we can see the minimization of the threat and the making of minimal assumptions about the audiences's needs in the structure of the stanza as definitional of deference politeness. The deference politeness strategy of giving the hearer the option not to get involved is exemplified in the verse structure as well as in the riddle genre. The examples we cited from Chief Henry's life story show in several cases the dissociation of the speaker and the hearer from the infringement involved. Thus the spokesman in suggesting what the group's activities should be uses a verb form without pronominal prefixes. He does not directly indicate to whom the suggestion is addressed, but only that it was said.

In our discussion of the Athabaskan stanza and other related communicative phenomena we characterized the stanza as an open structure. We see the Athabaskan stanza in its openness as a discourse reflection of the deference politeness strategy of making minimal assumptions about your listener's or audience's needs or wants and attending to them only as the need is expressed by them.

We have characterized open systems as resilient and stable over time. We have said that deference politeness, by being respectful of distance and of difference among individuals, is more tolerant of outside influences than solidarity politeness systems which emphasize the commonality of their members. Seeing Athabaskan communicative patterns as a deference politeness system, then, is consistent with the repeated observation that Athabaskan groups remain Athabaskan over many generations of change and cultural interaction with other groups. The distinctiveness of Athabaskan communicative patterns can be seen as a reflection of the openness and resilience of a deference politeness system.

ESSAYIST LITERACY AS
SOLIDARITY POLITENESS

The essential aspects of a solidarity politeness system are

a.   – P, an assumption of low power difference between members,
b.   – D, an assumption of low distance between members.

The fictionalization of the self is the key to understanding how essayist literacy is a solidarity politeness system. We have argued that central to essayist literacy is the fictionalization involved in authorship and readership. Chatman (1978) distinguishes between the real author and the implied author on the one hand and the real reader and the implied reader on the other hand. Essayist literacy is a system of solidarity politeness between the implied or fictionalized author and his counterpart the implied or fictionalized reader. These two entities are brought into a relation of solidarity politeness through the medium of the text. What is emphasized in essayist literacy is the common goals, attitudes, knowledge, and other attributes of author (implied) and reader (implied), whatever the actual relations between author (real) and reader (real) may be.

It is clear that there is distance in essayist literacy as in all communicative systems. In this case, however, the distance is between the real and implied roles. The distance is experienced not as mutual respect between individuals as in a deference politeness system but as alienation and fragmentation of the individual into multiple communicative roles.

The implied author and implied reader are in a relationship of low power difference and low distance in essayist literacy. The solidarity politeness strategies this implies are that the author will attend to the needs of the reader. He will indicate and even exaggerate his sympathy for the reader. He will use identity markers that will establish them as members of the same group. He will claim reciprocity, common knowledge and opinions. Generally, he will indicate his attention to the reader's needs and wants.

The explicitness of essayist text can be seen in this light as attending to the reader's needs. More important than attending to the reader's needs is that it makes a show of doing so. As is well known, when something is required for understanding of a point and the author is in doubt about whether the reader knows this background, he puts it in with a show. The phrase "as is well known" allows the author to tell the reader something he may not know without condescension (which would indicate high power + D) and also that he is going to assume the reader knows what he himself knows (assuming low distance − D).

Another clear display of common ground is the bibliographic reference. While a point may be wholly intelligible on the basis of the text itself, the "supporting" reference allows the author to show common membership in a community of scholars, a community of which the reader is also assumed to be a member.

It is important to reiterate that we are speaking of essayist literacy as a communicative style. At that level it may be characterized as solidarity politeness. This does not mean, of course, that within any particular example many other politeness strategies will not be used. For example, Brown and Levinson give nominalization as a deference politeness strategy. The presence of nominalization as a hallmark of essayist style has been observed in various places (S. Scollon 1979). We would say here that the presence of this negative politeness strategy at one level in what is a solidarity politeness strategy at a more inclusive level is not a contradiction but rather an example of the subtle mixing of strategies at what we might risk calling the tactical level.

We have said then that essayist literacy is a solidarity politeness system in the face relation between the implied author and the implied reader. The distance between real author and real reader may in fact remain great and be governed by deference politeness, solidarity politeness or even asymmetrical face relations. One can see, in the frequent observation that some author or scholar is in face-to-face relations a bore when in his writing he is so interesting, the mistake of taking real authors for implied ones.

The implication of viewing essayist literacy as a solidarity politeness system is that the groups of common membership established between authors and readers will be relatively unstable and short-lived. One would predict as one would also observe frequent changes in loyalty and the rapid growth and dissolution of "schools" or groups of common membership.

As an integral part of the modern consciousness, essayist literacy produces the pluralism so characteristic of that reality set. The alienation of the real and implied author and reader roles is one sort of pluralism that develops, the pluralism of communicative roles. The factions, schools, and other groups that result from schismogenesis produce a second kind of pluralism. In this respect the pluralism of roles and of knowledge in general of the modern consciousness can be seen as related to the view of essayist literacy as a solidarity politeness system.

A distinctly modern phenomenon is the "language crisis" experienced by writers and philosophers. The rejection of language by a Wittgenstein or the persistent wrestling with the sense of linguistic emptiness experienced by Beckett may be seen as related to the evolution of literacy in Europe toward solidarity politeness during the past two centuries. As it strives to express commonality and group identity, the language of solidarity politeness becomes less and less capable of the expression of difference. Because of the tendency to runaway increase of solidarity politeness, one sees the system tending to say more and more about less and less. What becomes central is expression of identity with a common group. We would argue that both the emptiness of much recent academic scholarly writing and the nonwriting or new nonliteracy of the generation now in public school are at least in part the products of essayist literacy. Because it is schismogenic and contains no internal negative feedback mechanism, essayist literacy carries within it as a system the seeds of its own destruction. The outcomes are a Murphy who saw nothing but symbols everywhere or a Watt who had not seen a symbol in many years.

The Mixing of Face Systems

We have suggested that the solidarity politeness of essayist literacy may operate against a background of some other system of real world relationships. We would like to emphasize that generally, as with speech acts in discourse, multiple strategies may be pursued in seeking to achieve the necessary interactional balance. While it is our view that deference politeness systems are more stable in themselves than solidarity politeness systems, we assume nevertheless that any speech community or other communicative group will make use of multiple strategies that will vary from context to context. In the case at hand in this study, it is our central concern to understand how two quite different communicative systems interact. We assume that the interaction that we describe for Athabaskan-English interethnic communication will hold for the interaction between any deference politeness system and any solidarity politeness system, whether they are characteristic of national, ethnic, age, professional, sex, or political groups.

Problems in Interactions Between Systems

Whenever two speakers interact they make sense of the interaction on the basis of assumptions they carried into the situation which are then sometimes reconsidered as the interaction continues. With the general theoretical considerations behind us, we would now like to look more closely at miscommunication to see to what extent considerations of face and politeness systems will help us to clarify the sources of difficulty. In this discussion to make things simpler we will assume a constant ranking of the imposition (R) and look only at power differences.

CASE ONE

In the first case we will look at what happens when the first speaker (S_1) assumes high power over the second (S_2). Distance is not particularly significant in this case. This situation may be symbolized by $+P \pm D$. This speaker assumes an asymmetrical system in which the hearer will respond with negative politeness or deference. He will use low-numbered strategies.

Everything works predictably if S_2 assumes $+P \pm D$. Both have assumed the same situation. Deference is shown and the interaction continues.

If for any reason S_2 assumes a low power difference, $-P$, there will be problems in the interaction. If he assumes $-P + D$, that is, if he assumes a deference politeness system he has no viable response to S_1's utterance. His only choices are to assume either that someone's assessment of the situation is wrong, or that he is being insulted. The basis of the insult will be either that S_1 has asserted high power $(+P)$ or low distance $(-D)$. Either would result in low numbered strategies such as "bald on record" and either would be heard as insulting to S_2 who has assumed $-P + D$.

If for any reason S_2 assumes low power and low distance, $-P - D$, he will respond with symmetric solidarity politeness. that is, S_1's utterance will fit his expectation for a low-numbered strategy and he will respond symmetrically in kind. S_1, however, has expected deference, a high-numbered strategy, and will hear S_2's response as an insult to his assertion of power.

In summary, if S_1 assumes $+P \pm D$ and S_2 does not the result will be either confusion or insult, or both. It may also result in an insult returned to S_1 before both speakers are aware that there is a disagreement on their assessment of their relative communicative positions. Of course, a perceived insult may easily confuse the possibility of renegotiation since one party or both has now a motive for maintaining disagreement.

CASE TWO

In the second case we will look at, S_1 assumes $-P + D$ governs their relationship. That is, he assumes a symmetrical deference politeness system. If that is the assumption of S_2, again, nothing goes wrong. The two will extend reciprocal deference politeness to each other and the interaction will be untroubled by matters of face.

If S_2 assumes $+P \pm D$, however, problems will ensue. S_2 will hear S_1's deference politeness as deference appropriate to his superior power and will reply with bald on record strategies. This of course will insult S_1 who has assumed a low power $(-P)$ relationship. They will need to work at reassessing this situation.

If S_2 assumes $-P-D$, he has no predictable response to S_1's deference politeness. It will sound as if S_1 is being standoffish. The two speakers will have to renegotiate their understanding. Again, this will be against the background of potential insult.

CASE THREE

We will consider the situation when S_1 assumes $-P-D$, that is, symmetric solidarity politeness in the third case. Where this agrees with S_2's assessment no problem will result from reciprocal solidarity politeness.

If S_2 assumes $+P \pm D$, S_1's solidarity politeness will be heard as exerting his power over S_2. S_2 will respond with deference politeness as he assumes is appropriate. This will not match S_1's expectations, however, and leave him with the choice of accepting S_2's high power designation $(+P)$ or renegotiating. Since he has assumed $-P-D$ it will be perceived as an insult to the closeness he has assumed to renegotiate either power or distance.

These situations of potential conflict can be displayed as in Table 5.

INTERETHNIC COMMUNICATION AS DIFFERENT FACE VALUES

In the three cases just outlined we have said that these outcomes are predictable whatever the reason for the difference in the assignment of P and D values. In the preceding discussion of Athabaskan-English interethnic communication we have suggested that Athabaskans on the whole assume a relationship of $-P+D$ between individuals. That is, Athabaskans assume that the difference between individuals must be respected and that this is best done by maintaining a high degree of interpersonal distance, particularly in encounters with strangers.

Essayist literacy assumes a relationship between implied author and implied reader of $-P-D$. As the integration of roles becomes more highly valued in America and Canada as a means of coping with alienation, there is a tendency for English speakers to assume in their "real" roles relationships of solidarity politeness.

Brown and Levinson mention western U.S.A. as a social world in which the assumption of $-P-D$ has become the norm. It is generally this individual that is most typical of what we have called "English discourse patterns."

In Athabaskan-English interethnic communication we can expect the situations in which $-P+D$ and $-P-D$ interact. Notice that from either direction there is simply no predictable or viable response. Any response of one to the other based on these interpretations of the relationship leads to either insult or the need to renegotiate or both. If the Athabaskan $(-P+D)$ chooses to maintain his high value on negative face $(+D)$, his only choice is to continue with deference politeness strategies. This leaves the English speaker with only the two possibilities of assuming the Athabaskan is standoffish or that he is showing deference to his own higher

Table 5
Sources of Problems (R assumed constant)

S_1 assumption		S_2 assumption		Result
$+P \pm D$ (asymmetrical)	bald on record	$+P \pm D$	negative polite-ness/off record	O.K.
		$-P+D$	(no response)	Disagree on P, insult
		$-P-D$	bald on record/ positive politeness	Insult to S_1's $+P$
$-P+D$ (symmetrical deference politeness)	negative polite-ness/off record	$+P \pm D$	bald on record	Insult to S_1's P
		$-P+D$	negative polite-ness/off record	O.K.
		$-P-D$	(no response)	D is wrong, standoffish
$-P-D$ (symmetrical solidarity politeness)	bald on record/ positive politeness	$+P \pm D$	negative polite-ness	Confuses S_1 about P/D
		$-P+D$	(no response)	P or D is wrong
		$-P-D$	bald on record/ positive politeness	O.K.

power. The perception of distance may feel like hostility to someone who assumes solidarity politeness. The acceptance of a high power relationship may be equally difficult.

On the other hand if the English speaker chooses to maintain his position of low power low distance ($-P-D$) he will continue to insult the Athabaskan because of the interference in his private world expressed by solidarity politeness.

Solidarity Politeness as Addictive

We have said that solidarity politeness is addictive (Bateson 1979). By this we meant that in granting positive face to the hearer the speaker at the same time claims positive face for himself. The system feeds itself through an escalating cycle of solidarity politeness. Now we would like to suggest that in conflicts between deference politeness assumptions and solidarity politeness assumptions there will be a tendency for the person assuming solidarity politeness to be somewhat blinded to the fact that something has gone wrong by his own assumption of common ground. As he uses this strategy to get into improved communication he will hear deference politeness returned. While this will go against his expectations, his solution will be to overcome this distance ($+D$) expressed by the other speaker with an *increase* in solidarity politeness ($-P-D$). As distance is still expressed by the other he may continue his attempts at escalation of solidarity politeness to remedy the situation. This is, of course, the situation we have described in chapter two of the English speaker talking more and more in an effort to get to know the other speaker. What we phrased there as "getting to know" the other we may now express as expressing solidarity politeness, or the assertion of common ground for interaction.

From the point of view of the other speaker who is using deference politeness strategies, it will be clear from one interchange that the assessments are wrong or in conflict. It will take only one more interchange to see that the other speaker intends to use solidarity politeness as an escalating solution. Very early in the interaction he has to make a choice between complete withdrawal or joining in the expression of solidarity politeness. It is this early dilemma that so often results in the Athabaskan taciturnity in interethnic communication as the only possible means of maintaining respectful distance in the face of an onslaught of solidarity politeness.

Individuals, Groups, and Contexts

Not every pair of individuals, of course, will consistently display patterns of their groups. Here we would like to emphasize that any individual may choose to maintain distance (− P + D) or to emphasize commonality (− P − D) with any other individual in some contexts. A person who has just suffered bereavement, for example, in many societies will choose (− P + D) for those outside his personal family realm. What we have spoken of as Athabaskan and English patterns are just an example of a more general pattern of relationships between − P + D and − P − D. Wherever these configurations of values appear, the communication between the parties involved may suffer.

A Preliminary Recommendation

While we will defer discussion of any extended recommendations until the end of chapter eight, here it may be useful to suggest how the potential of miscommunication may be minimized in situations where the interactants may approach with different communicative values. Because solidarity politeness tends toward schismogenesis, instability, and a certain blindness to other communicative strategies, we can suggest that solidarity politeness be avoided as an initial strategy. Deference politeness assumes distance between the parties and implies the recognition of the potential for difficulty. In doing so, deference politeness remains more sensitive to the ongoing flux of social interaction. Because negative face can only be gained by receipt from other interactants, it tends to bind the relevant parties into a pact of mutual respect and concern. We would argue that deference politeness, in fact, more accurately reflects the dynamics of the real situation of distance when strangers meet, or in the gatekeeping encounters we have mentioned earlier. For this reason deference politeness can be managed more successfully by participants who may expect difference in their initial communicative strategies.

EIGHT

CROSS-SYSTEM INTERACTION, ETHNICITY, AND COMMUNICATIVE PLURALISM

THE PROBLEM OF GIVENS

Power (P), distance (D), and the ranking of the imposition (R) have been seen as the principal determinants or "givens" of a system of face. In chapter seven we argued that whenever two speakers disagree about the values placed on P or D, and now we can add R to the statement, they will initially misunderstand each other's face intentions. This may lead to insult in some cases but will always lead to the need to renegotiate these values. In the renegotiation of the values of P, D, and R, someone will have to change his stance if the communication is to continue intelligibly.

While we suggested that English speakers and Athabaskans often differ in their assessment of the givens of P, D, and R, we did not get very specific about how these different assessments arise in the first place. In this chapter we will look more closely at the sources of the values P, D, and R and in addition to the question of contexts.

Three Sources of the Givens, P, D, and R

The first and most basic source of values for power, distance, and the ranking of the imposition is innate. The difference in power between full-grown, mature adults and young infants is obvious in virtually all species of mammals. We assume this to be no different for humans and certainly a first source of values for P. We can assume in the same way that gross and obvious innate differences of size, weight, strength, speed and so forth between humans give rise to immediate assignments of values of P.

A source of innate values for D may be assumed to reside in the obvious physical differences that are often glossed as racial differences or sex differences. A mammalian judgment of same group (closeness) or different group (distance) is a component of whatever ethical or moral judgments an individual makes about such differences.

Certain impositions are absolutely greater than others depending again on the innate physiological characteristics of the hearer. A request to pick up a five-pound object is different when directed to a two year old and to a strong, fully developed adult.

While we do not wish to make much of these innate factors, we would argue that ignoring them as contributing to facework is a more serious threat. For example, the solidarity politeness assumption of $-P-D$ in relations between, say, blacks and whites must somehow ignore or treat as trivial the fact that the potential source of high distance ($+D$) is present in some individuals of each group who display marked physical differences.

The fourth factor, context, becomes relevant here. Difference between two interactants is always and only perceived against some other background. Against the background of the mammalian world in general, the differences between human physical types are slight. In modern urban social life such differences can become central and dominate interaction.

A second source of the givens of P, D, R, and contexts for their interpretation we might call ecological. We mean to suggest by this that the conditions under which the life of individuals or groups is played out. In our discussion of Athabaskans we suggested that the need for a high degree of individual viability under extremes of isolation and environmental stress was a source of the high distance ($+D$) value that characterizes Athabaskan interaction. We also suggested that an academic conference might provide the ecological conditions under which low power low distance ($-P-D$) would be most viable.

A third source of the givens that govern facework is the socialization process. Teaching and learning in a particular group will involve both the manifestation and the inculcation of the group's given values. In chapter four we argued that the fictionalization of the self in authorship and the decontextualization from situational contexts of essayist literacy were taught through early patterns of socialized interaction. We argued in chapter seven that these characteristics of essayist literacy reflect a solidarity politeness relationship between implied author and implied reader. That is, essayist literacy implies a relationship of $-P-D$. These values of low power and low distance we have argued are inculcated and displayed in the child's early socialization to literacy. In chapter six we showed that the patterns characteristic of deference politeness, low power and high distance, $-P+D$, were taught in the early socialization to the bush consciousness.

In general then we see the givens of facework, P, D, and R as having three sources, an inate or biological source, an ecological source, and a source in socialization. It would be a mistake we argue to treat any one of these sources as the sole determiner of the givens. Facework in public interaction will always reflect all three sources to some extent.

The Circularity of the System

In our discussions in chapters four and six we argued that the teaching and learning styles of a particular group reflect the discourse patterns of that group. So with the introduction of the notion that the givens of facework are at least partly determined by the teaching and learning process we have come full circle from our beginnings.

We began by observing the potential for problems of communication when the patterns of discourse or communicative styles differed for two groups. We then argued that those discourse patterns were the reflections of face relations between the interactants. Those face relations we then argued were determined by the givens, power (P), distance (D), and the ranking of the imposition (R) and the contexts in which these are interpreted. These givens we then saw as partly determined by patterns of teaching and learning. Those patterns of socialization we saw in turn as at least partly determined by our original concern, the discourse patterns or communicative styles. The following sketch shows this circularity:

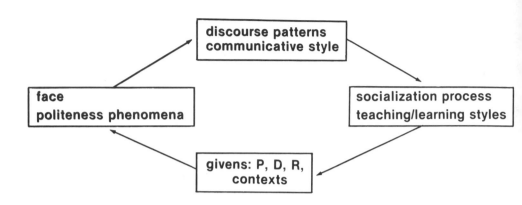

It is the circularity of this system that gives the stability and resistance to change so often observed in studies of patterns of communication, social relations, or teaching and learning styles. The system tends to reinforce itself, each element confirming the output of the others and in turn determining those elements. This circularity tends toward the closing of such a communicative system about a certain set of values and patterns of communication. If these were all there was to such a system we could expect separate, mutually closed systems to develop with boundaries across which no communication could occur. Of course, this is not the case, as we have already suggested in saying that the givens of face relations are only partly determined by the socialization process.

Other Determinants

If we sketched out our preceding discussion of givens it would look something like the following diagram:

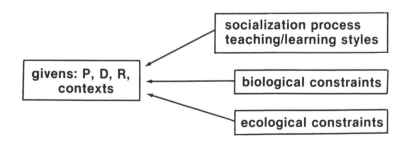

That is to say, the socialization process which in this case supports the circularity of the system is only one of at least three determining factors. The other two are presumably not influenced by socialization and therefore contribute other motives for the establishment of values.

At the same time we should observe that the givens of face relations determine things other than politeness phenomena in speech. We would argue that the whole concept of identity is tied to the values assigned to these givens. While face relations are public phenomena, one's identity is only partially public. These givens then, we argue, also determine one's private identity. In doing so they are highly influential over the totality of one's behavior whether it is carried on in public or not (Goffman 1979). A fuller view would be suggested by the following diagram:

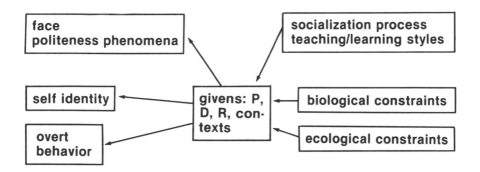

We have argued that politeness phenomena are jointly determined by the givens P, D, R, contexts, and by universals of face relations. A third determining factor consists of individual states. Whatever the givens are in a particular context, one's health, interest in the situation, or history in such contexts may all affect how facework is played out. For example, assuming even $-P-D$ in most situations, great fatigue may produce an assertion of distance, $-P+D$.

In addition we can say, again, that face determines more than just discourse patterns and communicative style. Goffman (1979) has shown how importantly body placement and clothing styles are determined by assumptions about face.

This element of the system could be more accurately shown then as:

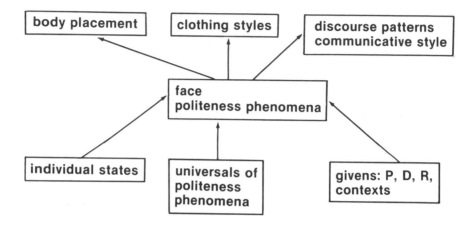

Discourse Patterns or communicative style are also determined by more than face or politeness phenomena. Significant among the determiners are the individual's knowledge of the various linguistic resources of his speech community. We might list knowledge of multiple codes, either languages or dialects, knowledge of motifs, formulae, idioms, generic structures, styles, and vocabulary among the significant resources that might be expected to limit or facilitate the speaker's expression in discourse.

Another element is the "story" (Chatman 1978). Not least among the determinants of one's discourse are the things one intends to say. Certain topics are more amenable to manipulation for face reasons than others. Some contents such as legends may be highly determined by historical traditions and must be passed on unaltered. In such cases the potential for face-motivated variation is quite limited.

Discourse patterns determine many things besides learning and teaching styles, of course. Sapir (1933) suggested the importance of the communication of ideas, the expression of personality, and the expression of membership in groups as significant functions of language.

This element in the communicative system then could be expanded as:

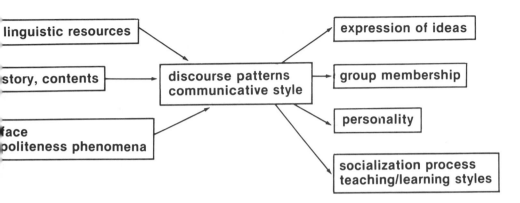

The socialization process is determined by factors such as communicative style but also by various traditions of teaching and learning that may in fact not necessarily relate to the system under consideration. This is certainly the case where the teacher is operating on the basis of professional training that requires different strategies from his or her own group's expectations. At the same time, the socialization process is determined by the individual's interests, capacities and such factors as age and maturity.

The outputs of the socialization process include more than the givens of face relations. To a considerable extent the knowledge and skills of individuals are outcomes of the teaching and learning process. This element then could be sketched out more fully, as:

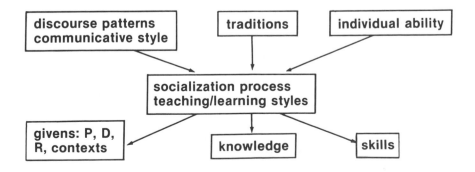

A Communicative System

The simple circular system with which we began was, of course, too simple. Now we have suggested ways in which the complexity of such a communicative system could be shown. In the following diagram we sketch out this fuller system.

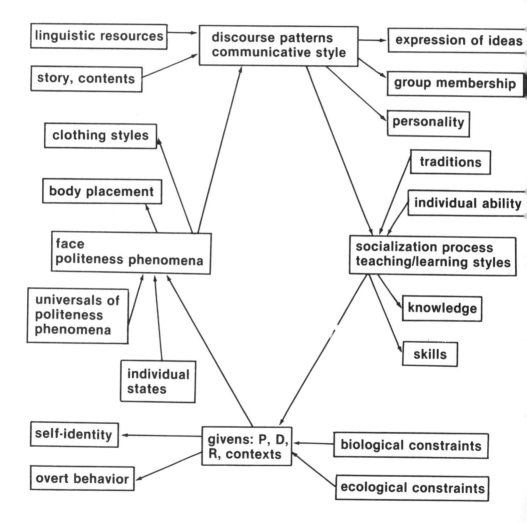

This admittedly much messier diagram of a communicative system we would argue is much closer to the truth than the simpler, closed system with which we began. The circularity and self-determining characteristic is still present as represented by the inner circle. It should be clear now that this inner loop is by no means all that is going on. The arrows drawn on the diagrams represent the direction of implication or determination. Because it is a circular system one could start anywhere. Explanations tend to be derived from working backwards in the opposite direction from the determination. Thus educators have begun with problems in the knowledge and skills of students. This has led into the element of socialization or teaching and learning. There the choice has been made differently in different cases. Some have looked to the individual ability of students as the explanation for educational failure. Because this explanation tends to reach a dead end very quickly at saying some are just smarter than others, educators have looked as well at traditions of teaching, curriculum development and assessment. Changes in those areas have not solved all of the perceived problems by any means and so other educators have begun to look back around the inner circle of the whole communicative system for explanation. This sort of explanation is more satisfactory in our view in two respects. It does not reach a dead end beyond which nothing can be done. That supports the hope that it is possible to provide equal educational opportunity for all students as our understanding of communicative processes improves.

The second reason this explanation is preferred is that it provides an explanation for the resilience of the system in the face of change. It becomes easier to understand why any major change in any such system will require a holistic approach to the system. Piecemeal adjustments to isolated aspects cannot be expected to alter much in the overall operation of the system.

Another area in which interest has been developing recently is that of communicative style. Here again, people interested in gatekeeping situations such as are involved in the employment or legal processes have seen communicative style as a significant determiner of success in such situations. Where explanations have been sought in the linguistic resources brought to bear on the situation there has been a dead end. The suggestion that some interactant lacked the grammatical or codeswitching tools for effective communication has been too simple. While there is certainly some such effect, we feel that it is important to consider the facework being done by participants if we are to understand how linguistic resources are brought to bear on communication.

Where explanations are sought it should be clear now that our preference is to look at the mutual determining characteristics of the whole system of communication. We do not of course suggest ignoring the other contributing determinants that we have outlined above. We do suggest though that the most productive understanding of communication and its consequences will be achieved by seeing each element of the system as mutually determined by and determining each other element.

ETHNICITY AS COMMUNICATION

Now that we have detailed the properties of a communicative system, we can give more substance to our concept of ethnicity as communication. An ethnic group consists of some such system with a closed internal feedback loop that maintains itself in the face of outside pressures for change. Such a communicative system is an ethnic group to the extent that it identifies this system with some historical, cultural, or even racial origins. These origins will ramify the internal circle of determinants by controlling as well ecological, traditional, and even biological constraints to the system. It will be able to maintain itself as a viable communicative system to the extent that the group as a group is able to control outside factors.

Interethnic Communication

We can define interethnic communication as any communication between members of two different communicative systems. Differences between the speakers could occur at any of the points of the system but are most likely to be re-established at all points. Because the differences are systematic there is the tendency for differences to be perceived as confirming one's own system.

To expand this point a bit, we can look back to the idea of explanation. If the question is why a person spoke in a particular way the answer, if it is one's own group, tends to look back around the circle. That is, my co-members speak the way they do "because that's how one speaks in such a situation" (face); if it is asked why they speak that way, it is "because that's how they are" (givens, identity); if it is asked why they are that way it is "because that's how they are brought up" (socialization); and if socialization is questioned the answer is "That's how we tell them to behave" (discourse patterns). In other words, *my* system makes sense in terms of system-internal determinants. It is natural to be the way one is, to speak that way and to teach others to do so. This perception of naturalness is the product of the internal and circular coherence of communicative systems.

It is different for others, however. In that case explanations tend to look into biological and ecological determinants. If it is asked why a member of some group X speaks the way he does, the answer is "because his grammar is limited." If it is asked why a member of another group speaks in a particular way in a certain situation the answer, again, looks to individual states. He is lazy, hostile, indifferent, aggressive, and so forth. If we ask about the givens of facework the answers look to ecological and biological determinants. They assert high power because they are innately aggressive. Finally, if we ask about learning capacity the answer is that they are suffering under some inherent limitations.

It has been argued by some that any particular communicative system will develop its own preferences for explanation. Selby (1975) has said that overall in America individual and biological solutions are advanced. In particular he suggests that attribution theory in psychology expresses a particularly American trait of looking to internal states and properties of individuals for explanations of behavior. He argues that Zapotecs on the contrary seek social explanations. Slama-Cazacu (1976) discusses the Marxist necessity of seeing the explanation of developmental phenomena as social at its foundation. We would argue that the ancient nature/nurture controversy cannot be discussed as only an intellectual issue. One's position in this controversy is in fact a significant expression of one's relation to a particular communicative network. The most "natural" position will in fact be the one most consistent with the internal dynamics of one's communicative system.

TOWARD IMPROVED
INTERETHNIC COMMUNICATION

We began this book by saying that we were concerned with problems of discrimination against ethnic minorities brought about by the interaction of those groups with the dominant technological and bureaucratic system of the United States and Canada. We argued that a significant aspect of this discrimination in the schools, in the legal system, in the employment and production system, and in the social services delivery system is the problem of communication. Communicative style is a major contributor to the outcomes of the encounter in significant situations such as gatekeeping encounters. Where the participants do not synchronize well the result is very likely to express itself as some form of discrimination against the nondominant members of the interaction—the student, the defendant, the employee, or the citizen.

With communicative style as a central focus we then went on to show that the face relations among the participants were critical in producing the interpretation of communicative difference. These face relations in turn were shown to be at least in part determined by socialization processes which themselves were determined at least in part by communicative style.

This circle of determination then was defined as a communicative system and we argued that interethnic communication was problematic because it is communication across system boundaries. We also have argued that there was a considerable problem involved in advocating change because of the internal consistency of separate systems.

What recourse to action does this view of communication give us?

First, because any change to be effective must encompass the whole communicative system, we recommend avoiding changes focused on any single element that do not take into consideration whole properties of the system. In general, changes focused on single elements of the system show themselves to assume explanations of the sort that dead end in biological or individual failure. Changes must look around the circle for effects in every other aspect of the system.

Second, any changes must look at all the systems that interact in a particular situation. In interethnic communication the communicative system of all participants must be seen as separate, interacting systems if the implications of change are to be understood.

Third, because of the complexity of any single system, and because interacting systems are even more complex, we must simply give up the illusion that change can be brought about through the unilateral action of any one side to the interaction.

Fourth, we cannot expect the solution of interethnic communication problems to lie in anyone's simple learning of "the other" system. While Erickson (1976) has shown that co-membership does override communicative style and it might be thought that by learning "the other" system one would achieve some degree of co-membership among participants, the learning of a communicative style requires a long and intense period of actual membership in the group. Where the participants in interethnic communication are communicating institutionally, as happens when a teacher, for example, teaches children who are culturally different, the displacement of the problem to some position internal to the teacher or the student does not strictly improve matters. If the teacher learns and uses the child's system the conflict remains, now in the relationship between the teacher and the larger system. Furthermore, in most cases where cultural or communicative pluralism exists it exists in abundance. A teacher has four or five separate groups with which to deal. A judge has fifty different groups represented before him in court. An employer has a dozen different minority group members as employees. No simple adoption of "the other" system can cope with this degree of plurality.

We believe the solution lies in the systematic differences between solidarity and deference politeness. While solidarity politeness emphasizes solidarity and commonality, it also is addictive in Bateson's (1979) sense and results in escalating schismogenesis. Deference politeness emphasizes distance, respect, and nonimposition. As a result it is stable or resilient and can weather internal variability and fluctuation. We suggest that any attempt at change of communicative systems that consists in the two parties to the change becoming more like each other is a change toward solidarity politeness. The risk is the instability of solidarity politeness systems. Solutions to problems of interethnic communication that emphasize solidarity politeness can only result in the loss of ethnic identity. There is a structural basis for the truism that ethnic difference cannot be preserved and respected by everyone becoming the same. We would argue further that ethnic assimilation simply cannot work because of the schismogenesis implicit in the system of solidarity politeness. It is no surprise that attempts at assimilation of ethnic minorities have only had temporary success. Structurally, ethnic assimilation is impossible.

Therefore we offer deference politeness as the most effective way of minimizing conflict in interethnic communication. We must assume cultural, ethnic, and communicative pluralism as the only solution that will produce overall resilience of the communicative system. Difference and the resulting distance are essential for system stability. Our recommendation then is that deference politeness be cultivated in all cross-system communication no matter what the internal properties of the respective systems are. Only by showing a profound and sincere respect for communicative differences can the overall system gain stability.

Then, since deference politeness is based on a low power differential ($-P$) and the respect of distance, we must educate ourselves to the value of all individual and group differences and treat them with genuine respect while maintaining our efforts to eliminate disparities of power between individuals and groups. This respect for difference at the same time must not fall into solidarity politeness by the cultivation of self-disrespect or disrespect of one's own group.

We believe that interethnic communication is not merely here to stay as a fact of the modern world; if treated with knowledge and respect for difference and the minimization of power differences, interethnic communication is our most positive communicative resource for both national and world stability.

Bibliography

Basso, Keith. 1970. To give up on words: Silence in the Western Apache culture. Southwestern Journal of Anthropology 26(3):213–230.

Bateson, Gregory. 1972. Steps to an ecology of mind. New York: Ballantine Books.

———. 1979. Mind and nature: A necessary unity. New York: E. P. Dutton.

Berger, Peter, Brigitte Berger and Hansfried Kellner. 1973. The homeless mind: Modernization and consciousness. New York: Random House.

Bloom, Lois. 1973. One word at a time. The Hague: Mouton.

Brown, Penelope and Stephen Levinson. 1978. Universals in language usage: Politeness phenomena. In: Goody, Ester (ed.), Questions and politeness: Strategies in social interaction. New York: Cambridge University Press.

Brown, Roger. 1973. A first language: The early stages. Cambridge, Mass.: Harvard University Press.

Cazden, Courtney and Dell Hymes. 1978. Narrative thinking and story-telling rights: A folklorist's clue to a critique of education. Keystone Folklore 22(1–2):21–35.

Chao, Yuen Ren. 1968. Language and symbolic systems. New York: Cambridge University Press.

Chatman, Seymour. 1978. Story and discourse: narrative structure in fiction and film. Ithaca: Cornell University Press.

Cook-Gumperz, Jenny. 1978. Interactive styles in instructional talk. Paper presented at the 77th Annual Meeting of the American Anthropological Association, Los Angeles, November 14–18, 1978.

Cook-Gumperz, Jenny and John Gumperz. 1978. From oral to written culture: The transition to literacy. Marcia Farr Whitehead (ed.), Variation in writing. Hillsdale, N.J.: Lawrence Erlbaum Associates.

Dauenhauer, Richard. 1975. Text and context in Tlingit oral tradition. Ann Arbor: University Microfilms.

————. 1976a. The narrative frame: Style and personality in Tlingit prose narrative. In: Stephen Mannenback (ed.), Folklore Forum: Special Issue "Trends and New Vistas in Contemporary Native American Folklore Study". Indiana University Bibliographic and Special Series, No. 15, Vol. 9.

————. 1976b. Riddle and poetry handbook. Alaska Native Education Board.

Erickson, Fred. 1976. Gatekeeping encounters: A social selection process. In: P. R. Sanday (ed.), Anthropology and the public interest: Fieldwork and theory. New York: Academic Press, Inc.

Faas, Ekbert. 1978. Toward a new American poetics: Essays and interviews. Santa Barbara: Black Sparrow Press.

Foster, Michael. 1974. From the earth to beyond the sky: An ethnographic approach to four Longhouse Iroquois speech events. Canadian Ethnology Service Paper No. 20. Ottawa: National Museums of Canada.

Foucault, Michel. 1973. The order of things. New York: Random House.

————. 1976. The archeology of knowledge. New York: Harper and Row.

————. 1977a. Discipline and punish. New York: Pantheon Books.

————. 1977b. Language, counter-memory, practice. Ithaca: Cornell.

Goffman, Erving. 1974. Frame analysis. New York: Harper and Row.

————. 1976. Replies and responses. Language in Society 5(3):257–313.

————. 1978. Response cries. Language 54(4):787–815.

————. 1979. Gender advertisements. New York: Harper and Row.

Goody, Jack. 1968. Literacy in traditional societies. Cambridge: Cambridge University Press.

————. 1977. The domestication of the savage mind. New York: Cambridge University Press.

————. n.d. Memory and learning in oral and literate culture: The reproduction of the Bagre. Unpublished paper.

Goody, Jack and Ian Watt. 1963. The consequences of literacy. Comparative Studies in Society and History 5:304–345.

Grace, George. In press. An essay on language. Columbia, S.C.: Hornbeam Press.

Gumperz, John. 1977a. The conversational analysis of interethnic communication. In: E. Lamar Ross (ed.), Interethnic communication. Proceedings of the Southern Anthropological Society, University of Georgia. University of Georgia Press.

_____. 1977b. Sociocultural knowledge in conversational inference. 28th Annual Roundtable Monograph Series on Languages and Linguistics. Washington D.C.: Georgetown University.

Gumperz, John and Celia Roberts. 1978. Developing awareness skills for interethnic communication. Middlesex, England: National Centre for Industrial Language Training.

Hall, Donald. 1973. Writing well. Boston: Little, Brown and Co.

Halliday, M. A. K. 1975. Learning how to mean: Explorations in the development of language. London: Edward Arnold.

_____. 1976a. Meaning and the construction of reality in early childhood. In: H. L. Pick, Jr., and E. Saltzman (eds.), Modes of perceiving and processsing information. Hillsdale, N.J.: Lawrence Erlbaum Associates.

_____. 1976b. How children learn language. In: R. D. Eagleson and K. Watson (eds.), English in secondary schools: Today and tomorrow. Sydney: English Teachers' Association.

_____. 1976c. On the development of texture in child language. In T. Myers (ed.), Proceedings of the First Edinburgh Speech Communication Seminar. Edinburgh: Edinburgh University Press.

Havelock, E. 1963. Preface to Plato. Cambridge, Mass.: Harvard University Press.

Hippler, Arthur E. and Stephen Conn. 1972. Traditional Athabascan law ways and their relationship to contemporary problems of "bush justice." Fairbanks: Institute of Social, Economic and Government Research, Occasional Papers No. 7, August 1972.

Holling, C. S. 1976. Resilience and stability of ecosystems. In: Erich Jantsch and Conrad H. Waddington (eds.), Evolution and consciousness: Human systems in transition. Reading, Mass.: Addison-Wesley Publishing Co.

Hopper, Paul and Sandra Thompson. 1980. Transitivity in grammar and discourse. Language, Vol. 56, No. 2:251–299.

Hymes, Dell. 1966. Two types of linguistic relativity. In William Bright (ed.), Sociolinguistics. The Hague: Mouton.

_____. 1971. The "wife" who "goes out" like a man: Reinterpretation of a Clackamas Chinook myth. In Pierre and Elli Kongas Maranda (eds.), Structural analysis of oral tradition. Philadelphia: University of Pennsylvania Press.

_____. 1975a. Breakthrough into performance. In Dan Ben-Amos and Kenneth Goldstein (eds.), Folklore: Performance and communication. The Hague: Mouton.

_____. 1975b. Folklore's nature and the Sun's myth. Journal of American Folklore 88(350):345–369.

_____. 1976. Louis Simpson's "The deserted boy." Poetics 5:119–155.

_____. 1977. Discovering oral performance and measured verse in American Indian narrative. New Literary History 8:431–457.

_____. 1978. The grounding of performance and text in a narrative view of life. Alcheringa 4(1):137–140.

_____. 1979. How to talk like a bear in Takelma. International Journal of American Linguistics 45(2):101–106.

Jacobs, Melville. 1959. The context and style of an oral literature. Chicago: University of Chicago Press.

Jette, Jules. 1913. Riddles of the Ten'a Indians. Anthropos 8:181–201, 630–651.

Jones, Eliza. 1979. Chief Henry Yugh Noholnigee. The Stories Chief Henry Told. Fairbanks: Alaska Native Language Center.

Kari, James. 1979. Athabaskan Verb Stem Variation: Ahtna. ANLC Research Papers, No. 2. 230 pp.

Kintsch, W. 1977. On comprehending stories. In J. Just and P. A. Carpenter (eds.), Cognitive processes in comprehension. Hillsdale, N.J.: Lawrence Erlbaum Associates.

Kintsch, W. and E. Greene. 1978. The role of culture-specific schemata in the comprehension and recall of stories. Discourse Processes 1(1):1–13.

Labov, William. 1972. The transformation of experience in narrative syntax. In: Language in the inner city. Philadelphia: University of Pennsylvania Press.

Leer, Jeff. 1979. Proto-Athabaskan Verb Stem Variation, part one: Phonology. ANLC Research Papers, No. 1. 90 pp.

Li, Fang-kuei. 1933. A list of Chipewyan stems. International Journal of American Linguistics 7(3,4):122–151.

_____. 1946. Chipewyan. In H. Hoijer (ed.), Linguistic Structures of Native North America. Pp. 398–423.

Li, Fang-Kuei and Ronald Scollon. 1976. Chipewyan texts. Institute of History and Philology, Academica Sinica, Special Publications No. 71. Nankang, Taipei, Taiwan.

McDonald, Robert. 1911. A grammar of the Tukudh language. London: Society for Promoting Christian Knowledge.

Mead, Margaret. 1977. End linkage: A tool for cross-cultural analysis. John Brockman (ed.), About Bateson. New York: E. P. Dutton.

Nelson, Katherine. 1975. The nominal shift in semantic-syntactic development. Cognitive Psychology 7:461–479.

O'Harrow, Stephen. 1978. On the origins of Chu-Nom: The Vietnamese demotic writing system. Lecture to the Linguistic Society of Hawaii, Mekong River Festival, May 1978.

Olson, David. 1977a. From utterance to text: The bias of language in speech and writing. Harvard Educational Review. 47(3):257–281.

_____. 1977b. The language of instruction: On the literate bias of schooling. In R. C. Anderson, R. J. Spiro, and W. E. Montague (eds.), Schooling and the Acquisition of Knowledge. Hillsdale, N.J.: Lawrence Erlbaum Associates.

Ong, Walter. 1958. Ramus, method, and the decay of dialogue. Cambridge: Harvard University Press.

_____. 1967. The presence of the word. New Haven: Yale University Press.

_____. 1977. Interfaces of the word. Ithaca: Cornell University Press.

Pawley, Andrew and Frances Syder. n.d. Sentence formulation in spontaneous speech: The one-clause-at-a-time hypothesis. Ms.

Peters, Ann. 1977. Language learning strategies: Does the whole equal the sum of the parts? Language 53(3):560–573.

_____. 1978. In and back out: Perception and production in language acquisition. Unpublished manuscript.

Playmore Edition. n.d. Goldilocks and the three bears. New York: Playmore, Inc.

Prigogine, Ilya. 1976. Order through fluctuation: Self-organization and social system. In Erich Jantsch and Conrad H. Waddington (eds.), Evolution and consciousness: Human systems in transition. Reading, Mass.: Addison-Wesley Publishing Co.

Sapir, Edward. 1933. Language. In: David G. Mandelbaum (ed.), Culture, language, and personality. Berkeley: University of California Press.

Schegloff, Emanuel. 1972. Sequencing in conversational openings. John Gumperz and Dell Hymes (eds.), Directions in sociolinguistics. New York: Holt, Rinehart and Winston.

Scollon, Ronald. 1976a. Conversations with a one-year-old: A case study of the developmental foundation of syntax. Honolulu: University Press of Hawaii.

_____. 1976b. The framing of Chipewyan narratives in performance: Titles, initials, and finals. Working Papers in Linguistics, Dept. of Linguistics, University of Hawaii 7(4):97–107.

_____. 1976c. The sequencing of clauses in Chipewyan narratives. Working Papers in Linguistics, Dept. of Linguistics, University of Hawaii 7(5):1–16.

_____. 1977. Two discourse markers in Chipewyan narratives. International Journal of American Linguistics 43(1):60–64.

_____. 1979a. Variable data and linguistic convergence: Texts and Contexts in Chipewyan. Language in Society 8(22):223–242.

———. 1979b. The context of the informant narrative performance. Canadian Ethnology Service, National Museum of Man, Mercury Series, No. 52. Ottawa.

———. To appear. The role of audience in the structure of Athabaskan oral performance. Proceedings of the XLIII International Congress of Americanists, Vancouver, August 1979.

Scollon, Ronald and Suzanne B. K. Scollon. 1979. Linguistic convergence: An ethnography of speaking at Fort Chipewyan, Alberta. New York; Academic Press.

Scollon, Suzanne B. K. Process orientation in Athabaskan Proceedings of the XLIII International Congress of Americanists, Vancouver, August 1979.

Scribner, Sylvia. 1979. Modes of thinking and ways of speaking: Culture and logic reconsidered. In Roy O. Freedle (ed.), New Directions in Discourse Processing. Norwood, N.J.: Ablex Publishing Corp.

Scribner, Sylvia and Michael Cole. 1978a. Unpackaging literacy. Social Science Information 17(1):19–40.

———. 1978b. Literacy without schooling: Testing for intellectual effects. Vai Literacy Project Working Paper No. 2. The Rockefeller University, Laboratory of Comparative Human Cognition.

Selby, Henry A. 1975. Semantics and causality in the study of deviance. In Mary Sanches and Ben G. Blount (eds.), Sociocultural dimensions of language use. New York: Academic Press.

Slama-Cazacu, Tatiana. 1976. The role of social context in language acquisition. In William C. McCormack and Stephen A Wurm (eds.), Language and man: Anthropological issues. The Hague: Mouton.

Tedlock, Dennis. 1972a. Finding the center, narrative poetry of the Zuni Indians. New York: Dial Press.

———. 1972b. On the translation of style in oral narrative. In Americo paredes and Richard Bauman (eds.), Toward new perspectives in folklore. Austin: University of Texas Press.

———. 1973. The story of how a story was made. Alcheringa, old series No. 5:120–125.

———. 1975. Learning to listen: Oral history as poetry. In Ronald J. Grele (ed.), Envelopes of sound. Chicago: Precedent Publishing, Inc.

———. 1976. From prayer to reprimand. In William J. Samarin (ed.), Language in religious practice. Rowley, Mass.: Newbury House.

Thompson, Chad L. 1979. Topicalization and pronominalization in Athabaskan languages. Paper presented at Alaska Anthropology Conference, University of Alaska, Fairbanks, April 6, 1979.

Toelken, Barre. 1969. The "pretty language" of Yellowman: Genre, mode and texture in Navaho Coyote narratives. Genre 2(3):211–235.

Tritt, Albert. n.d. [Journals.] Manuscript. Alaska Native Language Center, University of Alaska, Fairbanks.

Witherspoon, Gary. 1977. Language and art in the Navajo universe. Ann Arbor: University of Michigan Press.